W9-APU-045

Betty Crocker's

RED SPOON COLLECTION™

BEST RECIPES FOR
APPETIZERS

PRENTICE HALL PRESS

New York   London   Toronto   Sydney   Tokyo

Copyright © 1989 by General Mills, Inc.,
Minneapolis, Minnesota
All rights reserved, including the right of
reproduction in whole or in part in any form.

Published by Prentice Hall Press
A Division of Simon & Schuster, Inc.
Gulf+Western Building
One Gulf+Western Plaza
New York, NY 10023

Published simultaneously in Canada by
Prentice Hall Canada Inc.

PRENTICE HALL PRESS is a registered
trademark of Simon & Schuster, Inc.

BETTY CROCKER is a registered trademark of
General Mills, Inc.

RED SPOON COLLECTION is a trademark of General Mills, Inc.

Library of Congress Cataloging-in-Publication

Betty Crocker's Red Spoon collection. Appetizers and snacks.
p. cm.
Includes index.
ISBN 0-13-073057-2 : $9.95
1. Appetizers. 2. Snack foods.
TX740.B515 1989
641.8′12—dc19   88-26587
CIP

Manufactured in the United States of America

10 9 8 7 6 5 4 3 2 1

First Prentice Hall Press Edition

CONTENTS

INTRODUCTION

Appetizers

What is an appetizer? Traditionally, it is a tidbit that satisfies your hunger—just enough to keep you from eating a sandwich even though you know dinner is not far off. Appetizers (or "hors d'oeuvres" as they are also called) are meant to arouse interest in the meal to follow. At least, this used to be the role of the appetizer.

Appetizers and Parties

Today people are entertaining less formally than they have in years past, and an interesting selection of appetizers can even replace the meal. Frequently, invitations to parties now read "From 7 to 9 o'clock," and guests help themselves from passed plates or trays set on candlelit tables in a casual, convivial atmosphere. This is an easy solution to entertaining, without the worry of matching tableware or whether there are enough chairs to go around the dinner table.

If you are planning a party, see pages 101–102 for advice on beverages. You'll find tips that take the guesswork out of deciding how much and what to serve. As for your party food, first count the number of guests. Then, estimate five to seven appetizers per person, unless the party is to take place during lunch or dinner hours; if this is the case, plan on ten to twelve. Serve light fare in hot weather when appetites are on the wane and bring out the hearty food on cooler days when it's especially welcome. You will find appetizer "menus" for parties in the Red Spoon Tips section at the back of this book.

When entertaining, the tendency is to get caught up in a flurry of enthusiasm and be overambitious in making appetizers. It is all too easy to overextend yourself, toiling the day before or frantically assembling canapés alone in the kitchen while your guests wonder where you are. Don't try to dazzle them with more complicated recipes than you can comfortably manage at once, and allow yourself one last-minute recipe. It is more important, if your party is to last longer than an hour or so, to replenish serving plates as needed. Don't forget to check that you have enough napkins (two or three per guest), small plates and forks (if needed) and do set out little dishes for discarded olive pits, wooden picks and the like.

Serving Appetizers

One of the delightful things about appetizers is that they can be so attractive. Don't crowd them on huge platters. Arrange them so they can be seen and enjoyed. There is only one rule when it comes to garnishing plates or trays: Never use something that is inedible or poisonous that might be eaten by mistake. Fresh herbs, herb blossoms, small flowers and flower petals give a pretty air to a plate of hors d'oeuvres. Small flawless vegetables (such as baby carrots with their tiny fern tops or miniature pattypan squash) make handsome garnishes, too. You can tie up small posies of fresh herbs in slender ribbons or serve cheese on a bed of colorful leaves. Anything goes!

At the Table

There may be times when you want to begin your meal on a more formal note or make a more substantial meal. Then, a first course is just the ticket. From delicate consommé or crusty Oysters Parmesan to piquant Fettuccine with Four Cheeses, a first course can start things off deliciously.

Snacking

Appetizers aren't just for parties. There is a fine line between an appetizer and the all-American snack. Snacks, hors d'oeuvres, appetizers—call them what you will, they are welcome treats on any occasion. If you have a craving for something sweet, turn to page 89 for a selection of satisfying breads, muffins and scones.

In the following pages, you will find both classic favorites and more unusual delicacies. The photographs will give you some suggestions for serving your appetizers, and you can look to the Red Spoon Tips section for even more assistance. There you will find many presentation ideas and tips for decorating that look time-consuming but are really a breeze. We even help you cope with party emergencies (should any occur!) so that entertaining can be as much fun for you, the cook, as it's supposed to be. Here, then, are some of our best appetizers; we turn to them time and time again, and we think you will too.

THE BETTY CROCKER EDITORS

· 1 ·
DIPS

Dilled Dip

½ cup dairy sour cream
½ cup creamed cottage cheese (small curd)
1 tablespoon finely chopped green pepper
1 tablespoon dried dill weed
2 tablespoons mayonnaise or salad dressing
½ teaspoon Beau Monde seasoning

Mix all ingredients. Cover and refrigerate to blend flavors, about 1 hour. Offer a choice of vegetable dippers.

Crabmeat Dip

1 cup mayonnaise or salad dressing
½ cup dairy sour cream
1 tablespoon parsley flakes
1 to 3 teaspoons dry sherry, if desired
1 teaspoon lemon juice
½ teaspoon salt
⅛ teaspoon pepper
1 can (about 6 ounces) crabmeat, drained and cartilage removed, or 1 package (6 ounces) frozen crabmeat, thawed and drained

Mix all ingredients. Cover and refrigerate to blend flavors, about 2 hours. Serve with raw vegetables or toast rounds.

Ginger Dip with Apples and Pears

ABOUT 3 CUPS

1 package (8 ounces) cream cheese,
    softened
1 cup plain yogurt
1/4 cup honey
2 teaspoons crushed gingerroot
1 can (8 ounces) crushed pineapple,
    drained
1 tablespoon ascorbic acid mixture*
1/3 cup water
2 pears
2 red apples
1 golden apple
1 tablespoon finely chopped almonds,
    toasted

Beat cream cheese, yogurt, honey and ginger-root until creamy. Fold in pineapple. Cover and refrigerate to blend flavors, about 1 hour.

Mix ascorbic acid mixture and water. Slice pears and apples. Dip fruit in mixture to prevent darkening; drain. Just before serving, sprinkle dip with almonds; serve with fruit.

*Ascorbic acid mixture, used as a wash for cut fruit, prevents browning and preserves flavor. Orange or pineapple juice will also keep cut fruit from discoloring.

Deviled Ham Dip

ABOUT 1 2/3 CUPS

1 package (8 ounces) cream cheese,
    softened
1 can (4 1/2 ounces) deviled ham
1/4 cup dry red wine
3 tablespoons finely chopped dill pickle
1 teaspoon instant minced onion
1 teaspoon Worcestershire sauce
1/4 teaspoon instant minced garlic
1/4 teaspoon dry mustard

Beat cream cheese, deviled ham and wine in small bowl until creamy. Stir in remaining ingredients.

DEVILED HAM SPREAD: Refrigerate until firm, about 8 hours.

Guacamole

2 large ripe avocados, mashed
2 medium tomatoes, finely chopped
  (about 1½ cups)
2 jalapeño peppers, seeded and finely
  chopped*
1 medium onion, chopped (about ½ cup)
1 clove garlic, finely chopped
2 tablespoons finely snipped cilantro
1 tablespoon vegetable oil
Juice of ½ lime (about 2 tablespoons)
½ teaspoon salt
Dash of pepper

Mix all ingredients. Cover and refrigerate to blend flavors, about 1 hour. Tortilla chips make ideal dippers.

*Jalapeño peppers are small (about 2½ inches long), medium to dark green in color and with flavor that ranges from hot to very hot. They are available both fresh and canned.

Spinach Dip

2 packages (10 ounces each) frozen
  chopped spinach, thawed and drained
1 can (8 ounces) water chestnuts,
  drained and finely chopped
1 cup dairy sour cream
1 cup plain yogurt
1 cup finely chopped green onions (with
  tops)
1 teaspoon salt
½ teaspoon dried tarragon leaves,
  crushed
½ teaspoon dry mustard
¼ teaspoon pepper
1 clove garlic, crushed

Mix all ingredients. Cover and refrigerate to blend flavors, about 1 hour. Nice served with rye crackers, rice crackers or vegetable dippers.

Following pages: Ginger Dip with Apples and Pears

Mexi-Dip

½ pound ground beef
1 can (15½ ounces) mashed refried beans
1 can (8 ounces) tomato sauce
1 package (1¼ ounces) taco seasoning mix
1 small onion, finely chopped (about ¼ cup)
½ medium green pepper, finely chopped (about ¼ cup)
½ teaspoon dry mustard
¼ to ½ teaspoon chili powder
Sour Cream Topping (below)
Finely shredded lettuce
Shredded Cheddar cheese

Cook and stir ground beef in 10-inch skillet until brown; drain. Stir in beans, tomato sauce, seasoning mix, onion, green pepper, mustard and chili powder. Heat to boiling, stirring constantly. Spread in ungreased pie plate, 9 × 1¼ inches.

Prepare Sour Cream Topping; spread over ground beef mixture. Sprinkle with shredded lettuce and cheese. Nice served with corn chips.

SOUR CREAM TOPPING

1 cup dairy sour cream
2 tablespoons shredded Cheddar cheese
¼ teaspoon chili powder

Mix all ingredients.

Salsa Roja

1 can (4 ounces) chopped green chilies,
  drained
3 medium tomatoes, peeled and finely
  chopped (about 2¼ cups)
1 medium onion, finely chopped (about
  ½ cup)
2 cloves garlic, finely chopped
⅓ cup chopped ripe olives
¼ cup snipped parsley
2 tablespoons olive oil
1 teaspoon sugar
1 teaspoon salt
½ to 1 teaspoon crushed dried red
  pepper

Heat all ingredients to boiling, stirring constantly; reduce heat. Simmer uncovered, stirring occasionally, until slightly thickened, about 3 minutes. Cover and refrigerate to blend flavors, about 4 hours. Perfect with tortilla chips.

Salsa Verde

1 can (4 ounces) chopped green chilies,
  undrained
½ cup chopped green onions (with tops)
¼ cup snipped cilantro or parsley
¼ cup finely chopped green olives
¼ cup tarragon vinegar
2 tablespoons olive oil
½ teaspoon salt
½ teaspoon dried tarragon leaves
¼ teaspoon pepper
2 cloves garlic, finely chopped

Place all ingredients in blender container. Cover and blend on high speed until smooth. Cover and refrigerate to blend flavors, about 4 hours. Accompany with tortilla chips.

Following pages: Salsa Verde (left) and Salsa Roja (right)

Chive and Vegetable Dip

1 cup creamed cottage cheese
1 tablespoon lemon juice
1 tablespoon milk
¼ teaspoon garlic salt
½ to 1 cup shredded carrots, sliced
 radishes, chopped celery or green
 pepper
1 tablespoon snipped chives
½ to 1 teaspoon lemon juice

Place cottage cheese, 1 tablespoon lemon juice, the milk and garlic salt in blender container. Cover and blend on high speed, stopping blender occasionally to scrape sides, until smooth, about 2 minutes. Pour into small bowl; stir in vegetables, chives and ½ teaspoon lemon juice. Refrigerate at least 1 hour.

CHEESE-CHIVE DIP: Omit vegetables. Add 3 tablespoons shredded American or grated Parmesan or Romano cheese with the cottage cheese.

CHUTNEY-CHIVE DIP: Omit vegetables. Add ½ teaspoon curry powder with the cottage cheese. Stir in 3 tablespoons chutney and ¼ cup chopped salted cashews or peanuts.

Eggplant Dip

1 medium eggplant (about 1 pound)
1 small onion, cut into fourths
1 clove garlic
¼ cup lemon juice
1 tablespoon olive or vegetable oil
1½ teaspoons salt
Raw vegetable dippers

Prick eggplant 3 or 4 times with fork. Cook in 400° oven until tender, about 40 minutes. Cool. Pare eggplant; cut into cubes. Place eggplant, onion, garlic, lemon juice, oil and salt in blender container. Cover and blend on high speed until smooth. Serve with vegetable dippers.

· 2 ·

SPREADS AND PÂTÉS

Deviled Ham and Mushroom Spread

ABOUT 2 CUPS

2 cans (4 ounces each) mushroom stems
   and pieces, drained
1 tablespoon margarine or butter
2 cans (4 1/2 ounces each) deviled ham
1/4 cup chopped pecans
2 tablespoons mayonnaise or salad
   dressing
1 teaspoon prepared horseradish
1/4 teaspoon garlic salt

Cook and stir mushrooms in margarine in 8-inch skillet over low heat about 5 minutes; cool. Stir in remaining ingredients. Spoon into crock. Cover and refrigerate until firm, about 3 hours. Garnish with snipped parsley, if desired. Accompany with party rye bread.

Chutney Spread

ABOUT 1 CUP

1 package (8 ounces) cream cheese,
   softened
1/3 cup chutney, drained and chopped
1 teaspoon curry powder
1/4 teaspoon dry mustard
Dash of salt

Mix all ingredients. Refrigerate until firm, about 4 hours. Accompany with assorted crackers.

Ham-Chutney Rolls

1 package (3 ounces) cream cheese,
  softened
6 thin slices cooked ham
3 tablespoons sweet chutney

Spread cream cheese on ham slices. Dot each with about 1½ teaspoons chutney. Roll up from short side; cut into 1-inch slices. Cover and chill.

Tortilla Cheese Wedges

1 egg
½ teaspoon red pepper sauce
¼ teaspoon salt
1 package (12 or 12½ ounces) large
  flour tortillas (about 7 inches in
  diameter)
5 teaspoons mild taco sauce
1¼ cups shredded Monterey Jack or
  Cheddar cheese
⅔ cup sliced green onions (with tops)
¼ cup vegetable oil

Beat egg, pepper sauce and salt until smooth. Brush each of 5 tortillas with about 2 teaspoons egg mixture and 1 teaspoon taco sauce. Sprinkle each of the 5 tortillas with ¼ cup of the cheese to within ½ inch of edge; sprinkle with 2 tablespoons green onions. Top each with 1 tortilla, pressing edges firmly together to seal.

Heat oil in 10-inch skillet over medium heat until hot. Fry 1 tortilla sandwich at a time, turning once, until golden brown, 2 to 3 minutes; drain. Place on ungreased cookie sheet; keep warm in 200° oven. Repeat with remaining tortilla sandwiches, adding more oil if necessary. Cut each tortilla sandwich into 8 wedges.

Bean and Sesame Seed Spread

1 can (15 ounces) garbanzo beans,
drained (reserve liquid)
½ cup sesame seed
1 clove garlic, cut into halves
3 tablespoons lemon juice
1 teaspoon salt
Snipped parsley

Place reserved bean liquid, the sesame seed and garlic in blender container. Cover and blend on high speed until mixed. Add beans, lemon juice and salt. Cover and blend on high speed, scraping sides of blender if necessary, until of uniform consistency. Spoon into crock. Cover and refrigerate about 1 hour. Garnish with parsley. Try this spread with wedges of pita bread, crackers or vegetable dippers.

Mock Caviar

2 cans (4½ ounces each) chopped ripe
olives, drained
2 tablespoons olive or vegetable oil
1 teaspoon dried tarragon leaves
2 teaspoons lemon juice
¼ teaspoon red pepper sauce
1 small onion, finely chopped
1 hard-cooked egg yolk, sieved
1 tablespoon snipped parsley
36 Melba toast rounds

Mix olives, oil, tarragon, lemon juice and pepper sauce. Cover and refrigerate 2 hours.

Spread in pie plate, 8 × 1¼ inches. Top with onion, egg yolk and parsley. Serve with Melba toast rounds; garnish with lemon wedges, if desired.

Creamy Shrimp Spread

2 CUPS

1 package (8 ounces) cream cheese,
   softened
1 carton (6 ounces) plain yogurt
1 tablespoon snipped chives
1 teaspoon prepared horseradish
¼ teaspoon salt
1 can (4¼ ounces) small shrimp, rinsed
   and drained

Mix all ingredients except shrimp thoroughly. Coarsely chop shrimp; stir into cheese mixture. Cover and refrigerate 2 hours. Serve with bran snack toast, if desired.

Cajun Crabmeat Mold

3 CUPS

2 packages (8 ounces each) cream cheese,
   softened
2 tablespoons dairy sour cream
½ teaspoon salt
½ teaspoon paprika
½ teaspoon ground red pepper
¼ teaspoon garlic powder
¼ teaspoon ground thyme
1 cup cooked crabmeat
¼ cup finely chopped green pepper
Rye crackers

Beat all ingredients except crabmeat, green pepper and crackers in 2½-quart bowl on medium speed until well blended, about 1 minute. Stir in crabmeat and green pepper. Line a deep 1½-pint bowl with plastic wrap; press mixture in bowl. Cover and refrigerate until firm, about 3 hours.

Unmold on serving plate; remove plastic wrap. Garnish with chili peppers, if desired. Serve with crackers.

Curried Shrimp with Flatbread

ABOUT 3 CUPS

Flatbread (below)
1 package (8 ounces) cream cheese,
 softened
¼ cup dairy sour cream
1 tablespoon lemon juice
1 to 2 teaspoons curry powder
¼ teaspoon salt
1 can (4¼ ounces) tiny cleaned shrimp,
 drained
1 hard-cooked egg, chopped
3 tablespoons finely chopped green onions
 (with tops)

Prepare Flatbread. Mix cream cheese, sour cream, lemon juice, curry powder and salt. Spread about ¼ inch thick on 8-inch plate. Top with shrimp and egg; sprinkle with green onions. Serve with Flatbread.

FLATBREAD

9 CIRCLES

1 cup all-purpose flour
1 cup stone-ground whole wheat flour
⅔ cup cornmeal
¼ cup vegetable oil
2 tablespoons sugar
1 teaspoon baking soda
½ teaspoon salt
¾ to 1 cup buttermilk

Mix flours, cornmeal, oil, sugar, baking soda and salt. Stir in just enough buttermilk to make a stiff dough. Knead 30 seconds. Shape dough, ¼ cup at a time, into a ball; shape into flattened round. (Cover remaining dough to keep it from drying out.) Roll as thin as possible into 10-inch circle with floured stockinet-covered rolling pin or lefse rolling pin on well-floured surface. (Lift dough occasionally with spatula to make sure it is not sticking, adding flour as needed.) If desired, cut or score circles into wedges or squares with knife or pastry cutter.

Heat oven to 350°. Place circle on ungreased cookie sheet. Bake until crisp and light brown around edges, 8 to 10 minutes. Cool on wire rack. Repeat with remaining dough. Break into irregular pieces or along scored lines.

Following pages: Curried Shrimp with Flatbread

Salmon Mousse

1 can (15 1/2 ounces) salmon, drained
   and flaked
1 medium stalk celery, chopped (about
   1/2 cup)
1 1/2 cups half-and-half
1/4 cup chopped green onions (with tops)
2 tablespoons lemon juice
1 teaspoon instant chicken bouillon
3/4 teaspoon dried dill weed
1/4 teaspoon salt
2 envelopes unflavored gelatin
1/2 cup cold water

Place salmon, celery, 1 cup of the half-and-half, the green onions, lemon juice, bouillon (dry), dill weed and salt in blender container. Cover and blend on high speed until smooth, about 2 minutes.

Sprinkle gelatin on cold water in 1-quart saucepan to soften; stir in remaining half-and-half. Heat over low heat, stirring constantly, until gelatin is dissolved; cool. Mix gelatin mixture and salmon mixture. Pour into lightly oiled 4-cup mold. Refrigerate until firm, about 2 hours. Unmold on serving plate. Thin slices of baguette, lightly toasted, are a good choice to serve with this elegant spread.

Smoky Salmon Pâté

1 can (15 1/2 ounces) salmon, drained
   and flaked
1 package (8 ounces) cream cheese,
   softened
1 tablespoon lemon juice
2 teaspoons prepared horseradish
1/4 teaspoon onion powder
1/4 teaspoon salt
1/4 teaspoon liquid smoke
6 to 8 drops red pepper sauce

Mix all ingredients. Spoon into crock. Cover and refrigerate until firm, about 4 hours. Serve with rye crackers.

Italian Sausage Terrine

1 pound bulk mild Italian sausage
1 pound chicken livers
½ cup chopped onion
¼ cup all-purpose flour
¼ cup brandy
1 teaspoon salt
¼ teaspoon ground allspice
¼ teaspoon ground nutmeg
¼ teaspoon ground cloves
¼ teaspoon pepper
2 cloves garlic, chopped
3 eggs
½ pound bacon (about 10 slices)

Cook and stir sausage until brown; drain and reserve. Place remaining ingredients except bacon in blender container. Cover and blend on high speed until smooth, about 45 seconds; stir into reserved sausage.

Line loaf pan, 9 × 5 × 3 inches, with heavy-duty aluminum foil, leaving about 3 inches overhanging sides. Place bacon slices across bottom and up sides of pan, letting slices over-hang edges of pan. Pour sausage mixture into pan; fold bacon over top. Place loaf pan in shallow pan; pour very hot water (1 inch) into pan. Bake uncovered in 350° oven 1½ hours.

Remove pan from hot water; fold foil over top. Place weight on terrine. (An unopened 46-ounce juice can makes a good weight.) Press down firmly 2 minutes. Leave weight on terrine; refrigerate until firm, about 6 hours. Do not remove weight until terrine is completely cool.

To remove terrine, loosen foil from sides of pan and, grasping ends of foil, lift out; remove foil. Cut terrine into ¼-inch slices. Accompany with an assortment of crackers.

Mock Pâté de Foie Gras

8 ounces chicken livers
½ cup water
1 chicken bouillon cube or 1 teaspoon
  instant chicken bouillon
¼ cup chopped onion
¼ teaspoon dried thyme leaves
3 slices bacon, crisply fried and crumbled
¼ cup margarine or butter, softened
¼ teaspoon dry mustard
⅛ teaspoon garlic salt
Dash of pepper

Thaw chicken livers if frozen. Heat chicken livers, water, bouillon cube, onion and thyme to boiling in 1-quart saucepan; reduce heat. Simmer until livers are tender, 15 minutes. Cool; drain and reserve ¼ cup broth.

Beat chicken livers, reserved broth and the remaining ingredients on low speed; beat on high speed until creamy. Spoon into crock. Cover and refrigerate until firm, about 3 hours. Accompany with crackers.

CHEESE HORS D'OEUVRES

Onion-Cheese Puffs

1 cup water
⅓ cup margarine or butter
1 cup all-purpose flour
1 teaspoon salt
¼ teaspoon garlic powder
4 eggs
¾ cup shredded Swiss or pizza cheese (6 ounces)
1 small onion, chopped (about ¼ cup)

Heat oven to 400°. Heat water and margarine to rolling boil. Stir in flour, salt and garlic powder. Stir vigorously over low heat until mixture forms a ball, about 1 minute; remove from heat. Beat in eggs, all at once; continue beating until smooth. Stir in cheese and onion.

Drop dough by scant teaspoonfuls 1 inch apart onto lightly greased cookie sheet. Bake until puffed and golden, 20 to 25 minutes; cool.

FILLED PUFFS: Place 1 salted peanut, ½-inch fully cooked smoked ham cube or half of 1 pimiento-stuffed olive on each puff. Top with enough dough to cover. Bake as directed.

TOPPED PUFFS: Place 1 pimiento-stuffed olive or ½-inch-square cheese slice (⅛ inch thick) on each puff. Bake as directed.

Chili-Cheese Balls

ABOUT 6 DOZEN BALLS

1 can (4 ounces) chopped green chilies,
  well drained
2 cups shredded Cheddar cheese (8
  ounces)
1 cup all-purpose flour
¹/₂ cup margarine or butter, softened
¹/₂ teaspoon salt

Heat oven to 375°. Mix all ingredients. Shape into ¾-inch balls. Place about 2 inches apart on greased cookie sheet. Bake until set, 15 to 18 minutes.

Cheese Crunchies

ABOUT 5 DOZEN SLICES

1 jar (5 ounces) sharp pasteurized
  process cheese spread
²/₃ cup all-purpose flour
¹/₄ cup shortening

Beat all ingredients on medium speed 20 to 30 seconds. Divide dough into halves. Shape each half on lightly floured, cloth-covered board into roll, about 8 inches long and about 1 inch in diameter. (Dough will be soft but not sticky.) Wrap and refrigerate until firm, about 2 hours.

Heat oven to 375°. Cut rolls into ¼-inch slices. Bake on ungreased cookie sheet until light brown, 10 to 12 minutes.

CHEESE STRAWS: Heat oven to 350°. After beating dough, place in cookie press with star plate. Form straws on ungreased cookie sheet; cut into 3-inch lengths. Bake until light brown, about 10 minutes. Remove immediately to wire rack. Makes about 4 dozen appetizers.

Beer-Cheese Spread

1 pound extra sharp white Cheddar
  cheese, shredded
¾ cup beer
¼ cup margarine or butter, softened
1 teaspoon dry mustard
⅛ teaspoon red pepper sauce

Place all ingredients in blender container. Cover and blend on high speed, stopping blender occasionally to scrape sides, until smooth, 2 to 3 minutes. Spoon into crock. Cover and refrigerate until firm, about 4 hours. Let stand at room temperature 30 minutes before serving. Nice served with thinly sliced French bread.

WINE-CHEESE SPREAD: Substitute dry white wine for the beer.

Blue Cheese Spread with Walnuts

2 jars (5 ounces each) pasteurized
  Neufchâtel cheese spread with
  pimiento*
2 packages (4 ounces each) blue cheese,
  crumbled
2 packages (3 ounces each) cream cheese,
  softened
½ cup finely chopped walnuts

Mix cheeses until smooth; stir in walnuts. Cover and refrigerate until firm, about 4 hours. Let stand at room temperature 30 minutes before serving.

*Neufchâtel cheese spread is soft and white, with a mild flavor. It's similar to cream cheese, but it has less fat—it also has fewer calories.

Garlic Jelly with Neufchâtel

1 jar (10 ounces) apple jelly
3 or 4 cloves garlic, crushed
1 package (8 ounces) Neufchâtel cheese

Heat apple jelly over medium heat, stirring constantly, until melted, 5 to 7 minutes. Stir in garlic. Pour back into jelly jar. Cover tightly and refrigerate, turning over every 30 minutes, until jelled, about 3 hours. At serving time, pack cheese into crock. Serve with jelly.

Following pages: Dilled Dip and Cheese Straws

Fried Cheese Meltaways

Vegetable oil
1 cup variety baking mix
1/2 cup milk
1 egg
1 pound Monterey Jack, Cheddar,
* American, Swiss or mozzarella cheese,*
* cut into 3/4-inch cubes*
Variety baking mix

Heat oil (2 inches) in deep-fat fryer or saucepan to 375°. Beat 1 cup baking mix, the milk and egg with hand beater until smooth. Coat cheese cubes lightly with baking mix. Insert a round wooden pick in each cheese cube; dip into batter, covering cheese completely. Fry several cubes at a time, turning carefully, until golden brown, 1 to 2 minutes; drain.

Cheese and Apple Toasts

1 cup packed parsley sprigs
1/4 cup walnuts
1 tablespoon dried basil leaves
3 tablespoons olive or vegetable oil
1 tablespoon lemon juice
1/2 teaspoon salt
1 medium apple, cut into 16 slices
1 tablespoon lemon juice
1/2 baguette, cut lengthwise into halves
1 cup shredded Swiss cheese (about 4
* ounces)*
1/2 teaspoon freshly ground or coarsely
* ground pepper*

Place parsley, walnuts, basil, olive oil, 1 tablespoon lemon juice and the salt in blender container. Cover and blend on high speed, stopping blender occasionally to scrape sides, until mixture is the consistency of paste, about 5 minutes. Toss apple slices with 1 tablespoon lemon juice.

Place bread halves, cut sides up, on ungreased cookie sheet. Set oven control to broil and/or 550°. Broil halves with tops 5 to 6 inches from heat until golden brown (if bread arches in center, turn crust sides up and broil until flat). Spread parsley mixture over each bread half; arrange apple slices diagonally on top, leaving small space between each slice. Sprinkle cheese over apples; sprinkle with pepper. Broil with tops 5 to 6 inches from heat until cheese is melted, 3 to 4 minutes. To serve, cut between apple slices.

Chili Quiche Appetizers

1 can (4 ounces) whole green chilies,
  drained, seeded and chopped
2 cups shredded Monterey Jack or
  Cheddar cheese (about 8 ounces)
1 cup variety baking mix
1 cup half-and-half
4 eggs
1/8 teaspoon red pepper sauce, if desired

Heat oven to 375°. Grease square pan, 9 × 9 × 2 inches. Sprinkle chilies and cheese in pan. Beat remaining ingredients until smooth, 15 seconds in blender on high speed or 1 minute with hand beater. Pour into pan. Bake until golden brown and knife inserted in center comes out clean, about 30 minutes. Let stand 10 minutes before cutting. Cut into about 1¼-inch squares. Refrigerate any remaining appetizers.

Parmesan and Sesame Drops

1 cup variety baking mix
1/4 cup margarine or butter, softened
3 tablespoons sesame seed
3 tablespoons boiling water
1/4 cup grated Parmesan cheese

Heat oven to 450°. Mix baking mix and margarine. Stir in sesame seed and water until soft dough forms. Drop by scant teaspoonfuls into cheese; roll in cheese to coat. Place about 1 inch apart on ungreased cookie sheet. Bake until golden, 7 to 10 minutes.

CHEESE-ONION SNACKS: Omit sesame seed and Parmesan cheese. Stir in ¼ cup finely chopped green onions and ½ cup shredded Cheddar cheese with the water. When snacks are done, remove immediately from cookie sheet.

Following pages: Chile Quiche Appetizers

Gouda Spread

1 whole round Gouda cheese (8 ounces)
1 tablespoon milk
1 tablespoon dry white wine or apple
  juice
1 teaspoon prepared mustard
2 drops red pepper sauce

Let cheese stand at room temperature until softened. Make four 2½-inch intersecting cuts in top of cheese ball, cutting completely through plastic casing. Carefully pull back each section of casing, curling point over index finger. Scoop out cheese, leaving ¼-inch wall. Refrigerate casing shell. Mash cheese with fork. Mix in remaining ingredients. Fill casing shell with cheese mixture. Cover and refrigerate until firm, about 3 hours.

Let stand at room temperature 1 hour before serving. Garnish with parsley, if desired. Accompany with crackers.

Chive and Feta Cheese Triangles

30 TRIANGLES

1 pound feta cheese*
2 eggs, slightly beaten
¼ cup snipped chives
¼ teaspoon white pepper
1 pound frozen phyllo leaves, thawed
¼ cup margarine or butter, melted

Crumble cheese in small bowl; mash with fork. Stir in eggs, chives and white pepper until well mixed. Cut phyllo leaves lengthwise into 3 equal strips. Cover with waxed paper, then with damp towel to keep them from drying out. Using 2 layers phyllo at a time, place 1 heaping teaspoon filling on one end of strip; fold end over end, in triangular shape, to opposite end. Place on greased cookie sheet. Repeat with remaining strips and filling.

Heat oven to 350°. Brush triangles with margarine. Bake until puffed and golden, about 20 minutes.

*Finely shredded Monterey Jack cheese can be substituted for the feta cheese.

Note: Before baking, filled triangles can be covered and refrigerated no longer than 24 hours.

Parmesan Fans

1 cup margarine or butter
1 1/2 cups all-purpose flour
1/2 cup dairy sour cream
3/4 cup freshly grated Parmesan cheese

Cut margarine into flour until mixture resembles fine crumbs. Blend in sour cream. Divide pastry into 4 equal parts. Wrap each part and refrigerate until firm, about 8 hours.

Heat oven to 350°. Roll one part into rectangle, 12 × 6 inches, on well-floured, cloth-covered board. Sprinkle with 2 tablespoons of the cheese. Fold ends to meet in center, forming a square. Sprinkle with 1 tablespoon of the cheese. Fold in folded edges to meet in center. Fold lengthwise in half (as if you were closing a book). Flatten lightly; fold lengthwise again. Cut into 3/16-inch slices. Place on ungreased cookie sheet. Bring ends of each slice together to form a fan shape. Repeat with remaining parts. Bake until light brown, 20 to 25 minutes.

Brie with Almonds

1 whole round Brie cheese (4 1/2 ounces)
2 tablespoons margarine or butter
1/4 cup toasted sliced almonds
1 tablespoon brandy

Place cheese on heatproof serving plate. Set oven control to broil and/or 550°. Broil cheese with top 3 to 4 inches from heat until soft and warm, about 2 1/2 minutes. Heat margarine until melted; stir in almonds and brandy, if desired. Pour over cheese. Nice served with crackers or sliced fruit.

TO MICROWAVE: Microwave cheese on microwavable serving plate on medium (50%) until soft and warm, 2 to 3 minutes. Microwave margarine in glass measure on high (100%) until melted, about 60 seconds; stir in almonds and brandy, if desired. Pour over cheese.

Brie in Crust

2 cups all-purpose flour
2 teaspoons baking powder
1 teaspoon salt
½ teaspoon dry mustard
⅔ cup shortening
½ cup boiling water
1 tablespoon lemon juice
1 egg yolk
1 whole round Brie cheese (2½ pounds)
¼ cup chopped green onions (with tops)
1 egg yolk
1 tablespoon water

Mix flour, baking powder, salt and dry mustard. Mix shortening, ½ cup boiling water, the lemon juice and 1 egg yolk; stir into flour mixture. Cover and refrigerate until chilled, about 20 minutes.

Divide pastry into halves. Roll one half into 14-inch circle on lightly floured, cloth-covered board. Place circle on ungreased large cookie sheet. Remove paper from Brie, leaving outer coating intact. Place cheese on center of pastry circle. Sprinkle green onions over cheese. Bring pastry up and over cheese. Press pastry to make smooth and even; trim if necessary.

Beat 1 egg yolk and 1 tablespoon water in small bowl with fork until mixed; brush over top edge of pastry.

Divide remaining pastry into halves. Roll one half into 9-inch circle on lightly floured, cloth-covered board; trim evenly to make 8½-inch circle. Place on top of Brie (do not stretch pastry). Press with fingers to make a tight seal.

Roll remaining pastry ⅛ inch thick on lightly floured, cloth-covered board. Make pastry decorations, if desired: With small leaf and flower cutters, cut out desired number of leaves, each about 1½ inches long, and flowers. Brush pastry circle with egg yolk mixture. Arrange leaves and flowers around edge and on center of pastry circle. Brush leaves and flowers lightly with egg yolk mixture. Freeze uncovered no longer than 24 hours.

Heat oven to 425°. Remove Brie from freezer. Bake until golden brown, 30 to 35 minutes. Cool on cookie sheet on wire rack about 1 hour. Place on serving plate while warm.

Hot Camembert and Marjoram Spread

32 SERVINGS

1 package (4 1/2 ounces) Camembert
   cheese
1 package (8 ounces) cream cheese,
   softened
1/4 cup milk
1/2 teaspoon salt
1/2 teaspoon dried marjoram leaves
2 eggs
2 green onions (with tops), sliced
Paprika
32 thin slices French bread

Remove rind from Camembert cheese and let cheese stand until room temperature.

Mix cheeses and remaining ingredients except paprika and bread on low speed until smooth. Pour into greased 1-quart casserole; sprinkle with paprika. Bake uncovered in 350° oven until knife inserted 1 inch from edge comes out clean, 30 to 35 minutes. Serve with French bread.

Camembert with Smoked Ham

ABOUT 2 CUPS

8 ounces Camembert cheese, softened
1/2 cup margarine or butter, softened
1/4 cup half-and-half or milk
1 cup finely chopped sliced smoked ham
   (about 6 ounces)
2 tablespoons finely chopped green onion
   (with tops)
1/2 teaspoon celery seed

Mix cheese, margarine and half-and-half until smooth. Stir in remaining ingredients. Cover and refrigerate until firm, about 4 hours. Let stand at room temperature 1 hour before serving.

Following pages: Brie in Crust

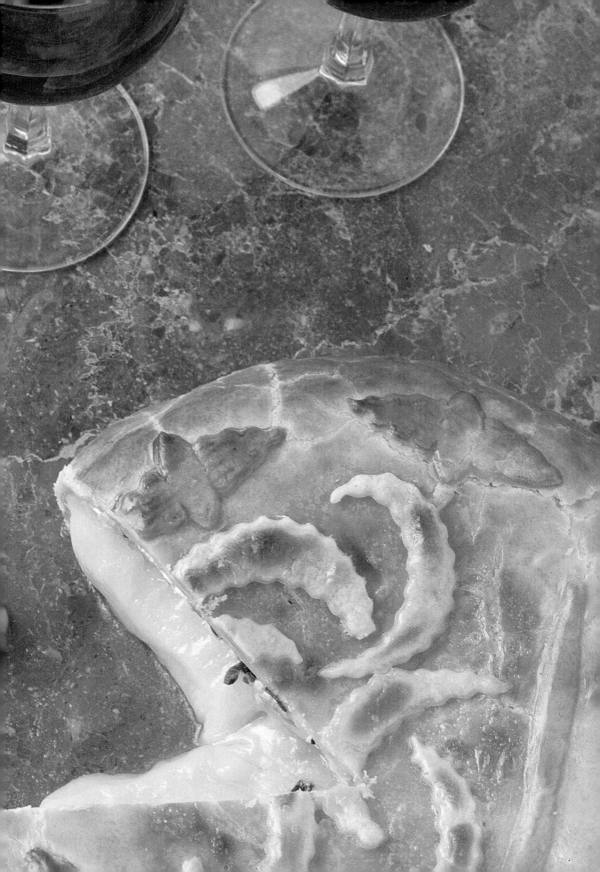

Salsa Cheese Bake

2 cloves garlic, finely chopped
1 tablespoon vegetable oil
1 jar (12 ounces) salsa
1 can (4 ounces) chopped green chilies,
    drained
2 tablespoons raisins
1/4 teaspoon ground cinnamon
1/8 teaspoon ground cloves
Dash of ground cumin
1/2 pound bulk Italian sausage
16 ounces Monterey Jack cheese, cut into
    1/4-inch slices
1/4 cup sliced pimiento-stuffed olives
1 package (12 ounces) round tortilla
    chips

Cook and stir garlic in oil in 1-quart saucepan until garlic is brown, about 1 minute. Stir in salsa, chilies, raisins, cinnamon, cloves and cumin. Heat to boiling, stirring occasionally; reduce heat. Simmer uncovered, stirring occasionally, until mixture is slightly thickened, about 3 minutes. Cook and stir sausage in 10-inch skillet until brown; drain. Stir in 1 cup of the salsa mixture.

Place half of the cheese slices in single layer in ungreased 1-quart shallow casserole or pie plate, 9 × 1 1/4 inches. Spoon sausage mixture over cheese slices in casserole; top with remaining cheese slices.

Bake uncovered in 400° oven until cheese is melted, 8 to 10 minutes. Heat remaining salsa mixture and the olives until hot; pour over cheese. Serve with tortilla chips.

Sesame-Cheddar Spread

2 cups shredded sharp Cheddar cheese
    (8 ounces)
2 packages (3 ounces each) cream cheese,
    softened
1/4 cup toasted sesame seed
1/4 cup half-and-half or milk
1 teaspoon soy sauce
1/2 teaspoon seasoned salt

Mix all ingredients until smooth. Cover and refrigerate until firm, about 4 hours. Let stand at room temperature 1 hour before serving.

Kielbasa in Fondue

8 SERVINGS

1 pound fully cooked kielbasa, cut into
  1/2-inch slices
2 cups beer
2 cups shredded sharp natural Cheddar
  cheese (8 ounces)
2 cups shredded natural Swiss cheese
  (8 ounces)
2 tablespoons all-purpose flour
1/2 teaspoon dry mustard
1/4 teaspoon pepper
1 clove garlic, cut into halves
1/8 teaspoon red pepper sauce

Heat kielbasa and 1/2 cup beer to boiling; reduce heat. Simmer uncovered 10 minutes; drain.

Toss cheeses, flour, mustard and pepper until cheese is coated. Rub bottom and side of 2-quart heavy saucepan or skillet with cut clove of garlic; add remaining beer. Heat over low heat until bubbles rise to surface. Add cheese mixture, about 1 cup at a time and stirring after each addition, until cheese is melted and mixture is smooth. Stir in pepper sauce.

Remove to ceramic fondue dish; keep warm over low heat. Spear kielbasa with long-handled forks; dip and swirl in fondue with stirring motion. If fondue becomes too thick, stir in additional heated beer.

Following pages: A lavish cheese board, shown with fresh figs and grapes. **Clockwise from top:** *Gouda (shown in its waxy red casing), Swiss, Livarot, Banon, Illinois Goat Blue, an American Camembert, Montrachet, Baby Chèvre with herbes de Provence, Wisconsin Cheddar, Monterey Jack with Red Pepper*

· 4 ·

SEAFOOD PICKUPS

Ginger Shrimp

1 ½ *pounds frozen raw medium shrimp*
4 *cups water*
2 *tablespoons salt*
¼ *cup soy sauce*
3 *tablespoons finely chopped gingerroot*
¼ *cup vinegar*
2 *tablespoons sugar*
2 *tablespoons sweet white wine*
1 ½ *teaspoons salt*
2 *to 3 tablespoons thinly sliced green onions (with tops)*

Peel frozen shrimp under running cold water. Make a shallow cut lengthwise down back of each shrimp; wash out sand vein. Heat water to boiling. Add 2 tablespoons salt and the shrimp. Cover and heat to boiling; reduce heat. Simmer 5 minutes; drain.

Place shrimp in rectangular dish, 11 × 7 × 1 ½ inches. Heat soy sauce to boiling. Add gingerroot; reduce heat. Simmer until most of the liquid is absorbed, about 5 minutes. Stir in vinegar, sugar, white wine and 1 ½ teaspoons salt; pour over shrimp. Cover and refrigerate 2 to 4 hours. To serve, remove shrimp from marinade with slotted spoon; sprinkle with green onions.

Shrimp-Bacon Bites

1 cup cleaned cooked shrimp (about 16)
½ clove garlic, slivered
½ cup chili sauce
8 to 10 slices bacon

Mix shrimp and garlic; pour chili sauce over mixture. Cover and refrigerate, stirring occasionally, several hours.

Cut bacon slices into halves. Cook bacon until limp; drain. Wrap each shrimp in bacon piece; secure with wooden pick.

Set oven control to broil and/or 550°. Broil with tops 2 to 3 inches from heat until bacon is crisp.

Shrimp Toast

½ pound fresh or frozen raw shrimp,
  thawed
½ cup chopped green onions (with tops)
¼ cup all-purpose flour
¼ cup water
1 egg
1 tablespoon cornstarch
1 teaspoon salt
¼ teaspoon sugar
¼ teaspoon sesame oil
Dash of white pepper
Vegetable oil
5 slices white bread

Peel shrimp. Make a shallow cut lengthwise down back of each shrimp; wash out sand vein. Cut shrimp lengthwise into halves; cut crosswise into halves. Mix shrimp, onions, flour, water, egg, cornstarch, salt, sugar, sesame oil and pepper.

Heat oil (1½ inches) in wok to 350°. Remove crusts from bread; cut each slice into 4 squares. Place 1 or 2 pieces shrimp with sauce on each bread square. Fry 5 squares at a time, turning frequently, until golden brown, about 2 minutes; drain. Cover and refrigerate no longer than 24 hours.

Heat uncovered in 400° oven until hot, 12 to 15 minutes; drain.

Following pages: Shrimp Toast

Crab Roll-ups with Avocado Dip

Avocado Dip (below)
1 can (6 ½ ounces) crabmeat, drained
*   and cartilage removed*
½ cup shredded Monterey Jack cheese (2
*   ounces)*
1 small zucchini, shredded (about ½
*   cup)*
¼ cup finely chopped celery
¼ cup finely chopped onion
3 tablespoons chili sauce
½ teaspoon salt
10 slices white sandwich bread*
3 tablespoons margarine or butter,
*   melted*

Prepare Avocado Dip. Mix crabmeat, cheese, zucchini, celery, onion, chili sauce and salt. Remove crusts from bread. Roll each slice to about ¼-inch thickness. Spoon crabmeat mixture across center of each slice of bread. Bring sides of bread up over crabmeat mixture; secure with wooden picks. Place roll-ups, seam sides down, in ungreased rectangular baking dish, 13 × 9 × 2 inches; brush with margarine.

Bake uncovered in 350° oven until golden brown, about 30 minutes. Remove picks; cut each roll-up into 3 pieces. Serve with Avocado Dip.

*Make roll-ups with regular thickness square sandwich bread, not extra thin bread.

TUNA ROLL-UPS WITH AVOCADO DIP: Substitute 1 can (6½ ounces) tuna, drained, for the crabmeat.

AVOCADO DIP

1 avocado, cut up
2 tablespoons mayonnaise or salad
*   dressing*
1 tablespoon lemon juice
½ teaspoon salt
⅛ teaspoon garlic powder
⅛ teaspoon red pepper sauce
1 tomato, finely chopped (about ½ cup)

Place all ingredients except tomato in blender container. Cover and blend on high speed, stopping blender occasionally to scrape sides, until smooth, about 1 minute. Spoon into small bowl; stir in tomato. Cover and refrigerate.

Escabeche

6 cups water
1 teaspoon salt
10 peppercorns
1 1/2 pounds red snapper fillets
1 medium red onion, thinly sliced and
  separated into rings
1 medium carrot, thinly sliced (about 1/2
  cup)
4 cloves garlic, finely chopped
1/2 cup olive oil
1/2 cup white wine vinegar
1/4 cup water
1/4 cup lime juice
1 teaspoon salt
1/2 teaspoon dried thyme leaves
2 small dried hot chilies, crushed
1 bay leaf
2 tablespoons snipped parsley

Heat 6 cups water, 1 teaspoon salt and the peppercorns to boiling in 12-inch skillet; reduce heat. Place snapper in single layer in skillet. Simmer uncovered until fish flakes easily with fork, 5 to 8 minutes. Cut fish into 1 1/2-inch pieces; place in heavy plastic bag or deep bowl.

Cook and stir onion, carrot and garlic in oil until crisp-tender; remove from heat. Stir in remaining ingredients except parsley; pour over fish. Secure top of bag or cover bowl and refrigerate 24 hours, turning occasionally. Just before serving, remove fish from marinade with slotted spoon; sprinkle with parsley. Serve with wooden picks.

· 5 ·

NIBBLES AND TIDBITS

Parmesan-glazed Walnuts

1½ cups walnut halves
1 tablespoon margarine or butter, melted
¼ teaspoon hickory smoked salt
¼ teaspoon salt
¼ cup grated Parmesan cheese

Spread walnuts in ungreased shallow pan. Bake in 350° oven 10 minutes. Mix margarine, hickory salt and salt; toss lightly with walnuts. Sprinkle with cheese; stir. Bake until cheese melts, 3 to 4 minutes.

Ginger Almonds

1 cup blanched almonds
2 tablespoons margarine or butter
1 teaspoon salt
½ teaspoon ground ginger

Heat oven to 350°. Place almonds and margarine in shallow baking pan. Bake 20 minutes or until golden brown, stirring occasionally. Drain on paper towels. Sprinkle salt and ginger over nuts; toss. Serve warm.

GARLIC ALMONDS: Omit salt and substitute garlic salt for the ginger.

Toasted Cereal Snack

4 cups toasted oat cereal
2 cups pretzel sticks
1 cup Spanish peanuts
¼ cup margarine or butter
1 tablespoon Worcestershire sauce
1 teaspoon garlic salt
1 teaspoon paprika

Mix cereal, pretzel sticks and peanuts in ungreased rectangular pan, 13 × 9 × 2 inches. Heat margarine until melted; remove from heat. Stir in remaining ingredients. Pour over cereal mixture, tossing until thoroughly coated. Bake in 275° oven, stirring occasionally, 30 minutes.

TO MICROWAVE: Mix cereal, pretzel sticks and peanuts in 4-quart microwavable bowl. Microwave margarine in 1-cup microwavable measure on high (100%) until melted, about 30 seconds. Stir in remaining ingredients. Pour over cereal mixture, tossing until thoroughly coated. Microwave, stirring every 2 minutes, until hot and crispy, 5 to 6 minutes.

Note: After baking, snack can be covered tightly and refrigerated no longer than 1 week or frozen no longer than 2 weeks. If frozen, thaw at room temperature.

Following pages: Ginger Almonds, Garlic Olives and Golden Mushrooms

Oriental-style Nuts

2 packages (3¼ ounces each) blanched
  whole almonds
1 can (7 ounces) dry roasted cashew nuts
1 teaspoon soy sauce
1 teaspoon water
2 tablespoons margarine or butter
1 teaspoon five-spice powder
⅛ teaspoon garlic powder

Place nuts in jelly roll pan, 15½ × 10½ × 1 inch. Mix soy sauce and water; drizzle over nuts, tossing to distribute evenly. Dot with margarine.

Bake uncovered in 350° oven 10 minutes. Mix five-spice powder and garlic powder; sprinkle over nuts. Bake uncovered, stirring occasionally, until golden brown, 8 to 10 minutes.

Parmesan-Curry Popcorn

½ cup margarine or butter, melted
⅓ cup grated Parmesan cheese
½ teaspoon salt
¼ teaspoon curry powder
12 cups popped corn

Mix margarine, cheese, salt and curry powder. Pour over popped corn; toss.

Golden Nut Crunch

1 can (12 ounces) mixed nuts or 1 jar
(12 ounces) dry roasted peanuts
¼ cup margarine or butter, melted
2 tablespoons grated Parmesan cheese
¼ teaspoon garlic powder
¼ teaspoon ground oregano
¼ teaspoon celery salt
4 cups honey graham cereal

Heat oven to 300°. Mix nuts and margarine in medium bowl until well coated. Add cheese, garlic powder, oregano and celery salt; toss until well coated. Spread in ungreased jelly roll pan, 15½ × 10½ × 1 inch. Bake, stirring occasionally, 15 minutes. Stir in cereal; cool. Store in airtight container.

SKILLET METHOD: Heat margarine in heavy 10-inch skillet until melted. Add remaining ingredients; stir until well coated. Heat over low heat, stirring occasionally, 5 minutes; cool.

Note: After baking, snack can be covered tightly and refrigerated no longer than 1 week or frozen no longer than 2 weeks. If frozen, thaw at room temperature.

Cereal Corn Snack

3 cups crispy corn puff cereal
6 cups popped corn
¼ cup margarine or butter, melted
¼ teaspoon onion salt
¼ teaspoon garlic salt
2 cups shoestring potatoes
1 cup French fried onions
⅛ teaspoon salt

Heat oven to 325°. Mix cereal, popped corn, margarine, onion salt and garlic salt in ungreased rectangular baking pan, 13 × 9 × 2 inches. Bake 5 minutes. Stir in potatoes and onions. Bake 5 minutes longer. Sprinkle with salt.

Garlic Olives

ABOUT 2 CUPS

1 can (7¾ ounces) ripe olives, drained
1 jar (7 ounces) green olives, drained
½ cup vinegar
½ cup olive oil
½ cup vegetable oil
1 small onion, sliced
1 clove garlic, sliced

Split olives slightly; place in glass jar with remaining ingredients. Cover tightly and shake. Refrigerate 2 to 3 hours. Drain before serving.

Marinated Mushrooms

ABOUT 2 CUPS

8 ounces mushrooms, sliced
½ cup olive or vegetable oil
2 tablespoons vinegar
2 tablespoons lemon juice
1 teaspoon salt
½ teaspoon dried basil leaves
¼ teaspoon dry mustard
⅛ teaspoon pepper
1 clove garlic, crushed
Snipped parsley

Place mushrooms in shallow glass dish. Shake remaining ingredients except parsley in tightly covered glass jar; pour over mushrooms. Cover and refrigerate at least 2 hours. Drain before serving; sprinkle with parsley.

Golden Mushrooms

1 pound medium mushrooms (about 24)
¼ cup chopped onion
¼ cup chopped celery
3 tablespoons margarine or butter
1½ cups soft bread crumbs
¼ teaspoon salt
¼ teaspoon dried marjoram leaves
¼ teaspoon pepper
⅛ to ¼ teaspoon ground turmeric

Remove stems from mushrooms; finely chop enough stems to measure ⅓ cup. Cook and stir chopped mushroom stems, onion and celery in margarine over medium heat until tender, about 5 minutes; remove from heat. Stir in remaining ingredients.

Fill mushroom caps with stuffing mixture. Place mushrooms, filled sides up, in greased baking dish. Bake uncovered in 350° oven 15 minutes.

TO MICROWAVE: Remove stems from mushrooms; finely chop enough stems to measure ⅓ cup. Mix mushroom stems, onion, celery and margarine in 1-quart microwavable casserole. Microwave on high (100%) until onion is tender, 2 to 3 minutes. Stir in remaining ingredients.

Fill mushroom caps with stuffing mixture. Arrange mushrooms, filled sides up and with smallest mushrooms in center, on 2 microwavable plates. Microwave one plate at a time on high (100%) 2 minutes; rotate plate ½ turn. Microwave until hot, 1 to 2 minutes.

Dilled Vegetables

½ medium head cauliflower (about 1
  pound)
½ pound green beans, washed and ends
  removed
1 small red onion, sliced and separated
  into rings
½ cup bottled Italian dressing
1 teaspoon dried dill weed
½ teaspoon red pepper flakes

Remove outer leaves and stalk from cauliflower. Cut off any discoloration, wash and separate into flowerets. Leave beans whole. Heat 1 inch salted water (½ teaspoon salt to 1 cup water) to boiling. Add cauliflower and beans. Cover and heat to boiling; reduce heat. Boil until crisp-tender, 6 to 8 minutes; drain.

Place cauliflower, beans and onion rings in shallow glass dish. Shake remaining ingredients in tightly covered container; pour over vegetables. Cover and refrigerate, stirring once, at least 4 hours. Drain before serving.

Vegetables in Crispy Potato Crusts

½ cup mashed potato mix (dry)
¼ cup grated Parmesan cheese
2 tablespoons margarine or butter,
  melted
½ teaspoon garlic salt
¼ teaspoon dried basil leaves
2 cups vegetables (fresh mushrooms or
  zucchini, cut into ¼-inch slices, or
  carrots, cut into ¼- to ½-inch slices
  or sticks)
1 egg, beaten

Heat oven to 400°. Mix potato mix, cheese, margarine, garlic salt and basil. Dip vegetables into egg; coat with potato mixture. Place on ungreased cookie sheet. Bake until light brown, 10 to 12 minutes. Remove immediately from cookie sheet.

Sauerkraut Balls

1 pound ground pork
1 medium onion, finely chopped
1/2 pound ground fully cooked smoked ham
1 cup all-purpose flour
1/2 teaspoon dry mustard
4 drops red pepper sauce
1/2 cup milk
1/4 cup snipped parsley
1 can (16 ounces) sauerkraut, rinsed, well drained and chopped
1/3 cup margarine or butter
2 eggs
1/4 cup cold water
3/4 cup dry bread crumbs
Mustard Sauce (below)

Cook and stir ground pork and onion in 10-inch skillet over medium heat until pork is done; drain. Stir in ham, flour, mustard and pepper sauce thoroughly. Stir in milk. Cook over medium heat, stirring constantly, until hot, about 5 minutes; remove from heat. Stir in parsley and sauerkraut; cool.

Heat margarine in jelly roll pan, $15\frac{1}{2} \times 10\frac{1}{2} \times 1$ inch, in 400° oven until melted. Mix eggs and water. Shape pork mixture into 1-inch balls; dip in egg mixture. Coat evenly with bread crumbs. Place in margarine in pan. Bake uncovered 15 minutes; turn. Bake until hot and golden brown, about 15 minutes longer. Serve with Mustard Sauce.

MUSTARD SAUCE

1/4 cup dairy sour cream
1/4 cup mayonnaise or salad dressing
1 tablespoon dry mustard
1/4 teaspoon sugar

Mix all ingredients until smooth.

Broiled Potato Skins

48 APPETIZERS

4 large baking potatoes
2 tablespoons margarine or butter, softened
1/2 teaspoon salt
1 cup finely shredded Monterey Jack cheese with jalapeño peppers (4 ounces)
4 slices bacon, crisply cooked and crumbled

Prick potatoes with fork to allow steam to escape. Bake potatoes in 425° oven until tender, about 1 hour; cool slightly.

Cut each potato lengthwise into halves; scoop out insides, leaving a ⅜-inch shell. Spread inside of shells with margarine; sprinkle with salt. Cut each into 6 pieces; sprinkle with cheese and bacon.

Set oven control to broil and/or 550°. Broil potato pieces with tops about 5 inches from heat until cheese is melted, about 2 minutes.

Jícama Appetizer

ABOUT 3½ DOZEN APPETIZERS

1 jícama (about 2 pounds)
Juice of 1 lemon (about ¼ cup)
1 teaspoon salt
1 teaspoon chili powder

Pare jícama; cut into fourths. Cut each fourth into ¼-inch slices. Arrange slices on serving plate. Drizzle with lemon juice; sprinkle with salt and chili powder. Refrigerate until chilled, about 2 hours.

Fruit on Skewers

30 APPETIZERS

1 small honeydew melon
1 medium papaya
½ pineapple
1 pint strawberries
¾ cup white rum
¼ cup honey
30 wooden skewers (about 6 inches long)

Scoop out melon and papaya with melon ball cutter to make 1-inch balls. Cut pineapple into 1-inch chunks. Remove green stems from strawberries. Place fruit in plastic bag. Mix rum and honey; pour over fruit. Secure top of bag and refrigerate 4 to 5 hours, turning bag occasionally. To serve, drain; place 1 honeydew melon ball, 1 papaya ball, 1 pineapple chunk and 1 strawberry on each skewer.

Fried Tortellini

Vegetable oil
1 package (7 ounces) dried tortellini
¼ cup grated Romano cheese
½ teaspoon garlic powder
½ teaspoon paprika

Heat oil (1½ inches) in deep fryer or 3-quart saucepan with basket to 375°. Pour ½ package tortellini into basket. Slowly lower into hot oil. Fry 1 to 2 minutes until golden brown; drain. Repeat with remaining tortellini. Mix remaining ingredients; sprinkle over warm tortellini in bowl and toss.

Creamy Tuna Garden Wedges

2 cups variety baking mix
½ cup cold water
1 package (8 ounces) cream cheese, softened
½ cup mayonnaise or salad dressing
½ cup sliced green onions (with tops)
2 teaspoons prepared horseradish
⅛ teaspoon red pepper sauce
1 can (6½ ounces) tuna, drained
2 medium stalks celery, cut diagonally into ¼-inch slices
Assorted fresh vegetables (sliced mushrooms, cherry tomato halves, chopped broccoli)
Shredded cheese

Heat oven to 450°. Mix baking mix and water until soft dough forms; beat vigorously 20 strokes. Pat dough in ungreased 12-inch pizza pan with floured hands, forming ½-inch rim. Bake until crust is light brown, about 10 minutes. Cool 10 minutes.

Mix cream cheese, mayonnaise, onions, horseradish, pepper sauce and tuna; spread evenly over crust. Divide dough into 6 wedges with celery slices. Top wedges with vegetables and cheese. Cover and refrigerate at least 1 hour. Cut into bite-size pieces or serve with small knife and let guests cut their own. Refrigerate any remaining appetizer.

Following pages: Jícama Appetizer

Mexican Deviled Eggs

2 DOZEN APPETIZERS

12 hard-cooked eggs, peeled
1/4 cup mayonnaise or salad dressing
1 jalapeño pepper, seeded and finely
    chopped
1 tablespoon ground cumin
1 tablespoon finely chopped capers
1 tablespoon prepared mustard
1/2 teaspoon salt
Chili powder
Snipped cilantro

Cut eggs lengthwise into halves. Slip out yolks; mash with fork. Stir in mayonnaise, jalapeño pepper, cumin, capers, mustard and salt; mix until smooth. Fill egg whites with egg yolk mixture, heaping lightly. Sprinkle with chili powder; garnish with cilantro.

Onion Twists

32 APPETIZERS

2 1/4 cups variety baking mix
2/3 cup milk
1 tablespoon onion powder
2 tablespoons vegetable oil
1 egg, beaten
Coarse salt

Heat oven to 425°. Mix baking mix, milk, onion powder and oil; beat vigorously 20 strokes. Gently smooth dough into ball on floured, cloth-covered board. Knead 5 times. Divide dough into 32 equal parts. Roll each part into pencil-like strip, about 12 inches long. Twist into pretzel shape on ungreased cookie sheet. Brush all twists with egg; sprinkle with salt. Bake until golden brown, about 10 minutes.

Party Sandwiches

CHEESE SANDWICHES

Sandwich bread
Whipped cream cheese (plain, chive or
pimiento)
Chopped or whole nut

Cut each bread slice into 3 rounds or 4 squares. Spread each with 1 teaspoon whipped cream cheese. Sprinkle with chopped nuts or garnish each with a nut.

CUCUMBER SANDWICHES: Cut each sandwich bread slice into 3 rounds. Spread each with $\frac{1}{4}$ teaspoon margarine or butter, softened, or 1 teaspoon whipped cream cheese. Fill each 2 rounds with a thin cucumber slice.

CUCUMBER-SHRIMP SANDWICHES: Cut each sandwich bread slice into 3 rounds. Spread each with 1 teaspoon whipped cream cheese. Top each with a thin cucumber slice, small amount of cream cheese and small cooked shrimp.

HAM SANDWICHES: Cut each sandwich bread slice into 2 diamond shapes. Spread each with $\frac{1}{4}$ teaspoon margarine or butter, softened. Mix deviled ham or chicken spread with small amount mayonnaise or salad dressing; spread over diamonds. Garnish with sliced pimiento-stuffed olives.

Note: To do ahead, place sandwiches on a cardboard tray; cover with plastic wrap. Overwrap with aluminum foil and freeze (up to 2 months). Forty-five minutes before serving, remove foil and let stand at room temperature. Do not add cucumber slices until just before serving.

Following pages: Party Sandwiches

Chicken Wing Drumsticks with Lemon Sauce

10 chicken wings
1 tablespoon cornstarch
1 teaspoon sugar
1 teaspoon salt
1 teaspoon soy sauce
1/2 teaspoon five-spice powder
Vegetable oil
1/2 cup all-purpose flour
1/2 cup water
1 egg
3 tablespoons cornstarch
2 tablespoons vegetable oil
1/2 teaspoon baking soda
1/2 teaspoon salt
Lemon Sauce (below)

Cut each chicken wing at joint to make 2 pieces (do not use piece with tip). Cut skin and meat loose from narrow end of bone; push meat and skin to large end of bone. Pull skin and meat over end of bone to form a ball; the wing will now resemble a drumstick. Mix 1 tablespoon cornstarch, the sugar, 1 teaspoon salt, the soy sauce and five-spice powder; sprinkle over drumsticks. Cover and refrigerate 30 minutes.

Heat oil (1 1/2 inches) in 3-quart saucepan to 350°. Mix flour, water, egg, 3 tablespoons corn-starch, 2 tablespoons oil, the baking soda and 1/2 teaspoon salt. Dip ball end of each drumstick into batter. Fry 5 drumsticks at a time, turning 2 or 3 times, until light brown, about 5 minutes; drain. Increase oil temperature to 375°. Fry drumsticks again, all at one time, until golden brown, about 2 minutes; drain. Serve with Lemon Sauce.

Note: After frying, drumsticks can be covered and refrigerated no longer than 2 hours. To serve, heat in 450° oven about 12 minutes.

LEMON SAUCE

1/4 cup chicken broth or water
2 tablespoons lemon juice
2 tablespoons honey
1 tablespoon vinegar
1 tablespoon vegetable oil
1 1/2 teaspoons catsup
1/4 teaspoon garlic salt
1 teaspoon cornstarch
1 teaspoon cold water

Heat chicken broth, lemon juice, honey, vine-gar, oil, catsup and garlic salt to boiling in 1-quart saucepan. Mix cornstarch and water; stir into broth mixture. Heat to boiling, stirring constantly. Cover and refrigerate if not serving immediately.

Mini Oriental Rolls

8 ounces bean sprouts (about 4 cups)
1 pound ground pork
1/2 cup chopped mushrooms
1/4 cup chopped water chestnuts
1/4 cup sliced green onions (with tops)
1 teaspoon cornstarch
1 teaspoon five-spice powder
1 teaspoon soy sauce
1/2 teaspoon salt
8 frozen phyllo sheets, thawed
2 tablespoons margarine or butter,
  melted
Hot Mustard (page 72)

Rinse bean sprouts under running cold water; drain. Cook and stir ground pork in 10-inch skillet until brown; drain. Stir in bean sprouts, mushrooms, water chestnuts and onions; cook and stir 2 minutes. Stir in cornstarch, five-spice powder, soy sauce and salt.

Cut stack of phyllo sheets lengthwise into halves. Cut each half crosswise into thirds to make 24 squares, each 5 1/2 × 5 1/4 inches. Cover squares with waxed paper, then with damp towel to prevent them from drying out.

Heat oven to 350°. For each roll, use 2 phyllo squares. Place about 2 tablespoons pork mixture slightly below center of square. Fold corner of square closest to filling over filling, tucking point under filling. Fold in and overlap the two opposite corners. Roll up; place seam side down on greased cookie sheet. Repeat with remaining phyllo squares. Brush rolls with margarine. Bake until golden brown, about 25 minutes. Serve with Hot Mustard.

Note: To do ahead, place rolls on greased cookie sheet. Cover tightly with plastic wrap. Refrigerate no longer than 3 hours. Brush rolls with margarine. Bake at 350° until golden brown, about 25 minutes.

Oriental-style Franks

1 tablespoon water
1 tablespoon soy sauce
1 tablespoon honey
2 teaspoons sugar
1/2 teaspoon cornstarch
1/8 teaspoon garlic powder
1/8 teaspoon ground ginger
1 package (10 ounces) frankfurters, cut
  into 1/4-inch diagonal slices
1 tablespoon vegetable oil
1 green onion, thinly sliced

Mix water, soy sauce, honey, sugar, cornstarch, garlic powder and ginger. Cook frankfurters in oil just until edges begin to curl. Stir in soy sauce mixture. Cook, stirring constantly, until mixture thickens and frankfurters are evenly coated. Stir in onion.

Chinese-style Barbecued Ribs

2 1/2- to 3-pound rack fresh pork back
  ribs, cut lengthwise across bones into
  halves
1/2 cup catsup
2 tablespoons sugar
1 tablespoon salt
2 tablespoons Hoisin sauce
1 tablespoon dry white wine
2 large cloves garlic, finely chopped
Hot Mustard (below)

Trim fat and remove membranes from ribs; place ribs in shallow glass dish. Mix remaining ingredients except Hot Mustard. Pour mixture over ribs; turn ribs. Cover and refrigerate at least 2 hours.

Place ribs in single layer on rack in roasting pan; brush with sauce. Bake uncovered in 400° oven 30 minutes. Turn ribs; brush with sauce. Reduce oven temperature to 375° if ribs are thin. Bake uncovered until done, about 30 minutes longer. Cut between each rib; serve with Hot Mustard, if desired.

HOT MUSTARD

1/4 cup dry mustard
3 tablespoons cold water

Stir dry mustard and water together until smooth. Let stand 5 minutes before serving.

Swedish Meatballs

½ pound ground beef
½ pound ground veal
½ pound ground pork
¼ cup dry bread crumbs
¼ cup finely chopped onion
¼ cup half-and-half
3 tablespoons snipped parsley
1 teaspoon salt
1 teaspoon Worcestershire sauce
¼ teaspoon ground allspice
½ teaspoon grated lemon peel
2 eggs
Sour Cream Sauce (below)

Mix all ingredients except Sour Cream Sauce. Shape into 1¼-inch balls. Place meatballs on rack in broiler pan. Bake in 375° oven until brown, 20 to 25 minutes; keep warm. Prepare sauce; pour over meatballs. Serve hot.

SOUR CREAM SAUCE

3 tablespoons margarine or butter
3 tablespoons all-purpose flour
1½ cups beef broth
1½ teaspoons dried dill weed
¼ teaspoon salt
¼ teaspoon ground nutmeg
½ cup dairy sour cream

Heat margarine in 1-quart saucepan over low heat until melted. Stir in flour. Cook, stirring constantly, until smooth and bubbly; remove from heat. Stir in broth, dill weed, salt and nutmeg. Heat to boiling, stirring constantly. Boil and stir 1 minute; remove from heat. Stir in sour cream.

Following pages: Chinese-style Barbecued Ribs with Hot Mustard

· 6 ·

FIRST COURSES

Melon and Prosciutto

*1 cantaloupe, casaba, honeydew or
  Spanish melon (about 3 pounds)*
*¼ pound thinly sliced prosciutto (Italian
  ham)*

Cut melon lengthwise into halves; scoop out seeds and fibers. Cut each half lengthwise into 6 wedges; remove rind. Cut crosswise slits 1½ inches apart in each melon wedge.

Cut prosciutto into 1-inch strips. Place several strips prosciutto over each wedge; push prosciutto into slits.

MELON AND PROSCIUTTO BITS: Cut melon into bite-size pieces. Wrap each piece in strip of prosciutto; secure with wooden pick.

Sparkling Fruit Compote

8 TO 10 SERVINGS

3 medium peaches
2 cups sliced strawberries
2 cups blueberries
2 cups melon balls
3 medium bananas
*1 bottle (1 pint 9 ounces) pink sparkling
  Catawba grape juice, chilled*

Peel peaches and slice into bowl. Top peach slices with strawberries, blueberries and melon balls. Cover tightly and chill.

Just before serving, peel bananas and slice into fruit mixture. Pour grape juice over fruit.

Oysters Parmesan

Rock salt
12 medium oysters in shells*
1/4 cup dairy sour cream
1/2 cup grated Parmesan cheese
1/4 cup cracker crumbs
1/4 cup margarine or butter, melted
1/2 teaspoon dry mustard

Heat oven to 450°. Fill 2 pie plates, 9 × 1¼ inches, ½ inch deep with rock salt (about 2 cups in each plate). Force a table knife or shucking knife between oyster shell at broken end; pull halves of shell apart. Place oyster on deep half of shell; discard other half. Arrange filled shells on rock salt base. Spoon 1 teaspoon sour cream onto oyster in each shell. Mix remaining ingredients; spoon about 2 teaspoons cheese mixture onto each oyster. Bake until hot and bubbly, about 10 minutes.

TO MICROWAVE: Fill 2 microwavable pie plates, 9 × 1¼ inches, ½ inch deep with rock salt (about 2 cups in each plate). Continue as directed, except arrange filled shells in circle on rock salt. Microwave one plate at a time on high (100%) 1 minute; rotate pie plate ½ turn. Microwave until oysters are hot and bubbly, 1½ to 2½ minutes longer. (If desired, oysters can be microwaved without rock salt. Decrease microwave time by 1 minute.)

*Opening Oysters: Scrub the oysters in their shells in cold water. Arrange six at a time on a microwavable plate, facing the hinges of the oysters toward the edge of the plate. Cover tightly with plastic wrap; microwave on high (100%) until the shells open slightly, 1 to 1½ minutes. Remove the oysters as soon as the shells start to open.

To open, hold the oyster with the hinge toward you and insert the blade of an oyster knife or table knife between the halves of the shell near the hinge; twist knife to force the shell apart.

Following pages: Oysters Parmesan

Mexican-style Shrimp Cocktail

24 fresh or frozen raw medium shrimp
1 cup water
Juice of 2 limes
1 clove garlic, finely chopped
2 teaspoons salt
Dash of pepper
1/4 cup chopped tomato
1 small avocado, chopped
2 jalapeño peppers, seeded and finely chopped
2 tablespoons chopped onion
2 tablespoons finely chopped carrot
2 tablespoons snipped cilantro
2 tablespoons olive or vegetable oil
1 1/2 cups finely shredded lettuce
Lemon or lime wedges

Peel shrimp. (If shrimp are frozen, do not thaw; peel under running cold water.) Make a shallow cut lengthwise down back of each shrimp; wash out sand vein. Heat water, lime juice, garlic, salt and pepper to boiling in 4-quart Dutch oven; reduce heat. Simmer uncovered until reduced to 2/3 cup. Add shrimp. Cover and simmer 3 minutes; do not overcook. Immediately remove shrimp from liquid with slotted spoon and place in bowl of iced water. Simmer liquid until reduced to 2 tablespoons.

Mix liquid, shrimp and remaining ingredients except lettuce and lemon wedges in glass bowl. Cover and refrigerate at least 1 hour.

Just before serving, place 1/4 cup lettuce on each of 6 dishes. Divide shrimp mixture among dishes; garnish with lemon wedges.

Artichokes with Garlic Dressing

6 SERVINGS

6 small artichokes
8 cups water
¼ cup vegetable oil
2 tablespoons lemon juice
1 teaspoon salt
½ cup chopped green onions (with tops)
⅔ cup olive or vegetable oil
⅓ cup tarragon vinegar
2 tablespoons chili sauce
1 teaspoon salt
1 teaspoon dried tarragon leaves,
* crushed*
¼ teaspoon pepper
2 cloves garlic, crushed

Remove any discolored leaves and the small leaves at base of each artichoke; trim stem even with base of artichoke. Cutting straight across, slice 1 inch off top; discard top. Snip off points of remaining leaves with scissors.

Heat water, ¼ cup oil, the lemon juice and 1 teaspoon salt to boiling in 4-quart Dutch oven. Add artichokes. Heat to boiling; reduce heat. Cover and simmer until leaves pull out easily and bottom is tender when pierced with a fork, 30 to 40 minutes. Carefully remove artichokes from water (use tongs or two large spoons). Place upside down to drain; cool.

Gently spread leaves apart and remove choke from center of each artichoke with metal spoon. Sprinkle green onions into centers. Shake ⅔ cup oil, the vinegar, chili sauce, 1 teaspoon salt, the tarragon, pepper and garlic in tightly covered glass jar; pour into artichokes. Cover and refrigerate at least 12 hours.

Serve artichokes with dressing in center. When eating, pull leaves from inside to outside to distribute dressing.

Asparagus Spears with Maltaise Sauce

6 SERVINGS

2 cans (15 ounces each) asparagus
   spears, drained
2 egg yolks
2 tablespoons plain yogurt
1 tablespoon lemon juice
½ cup margarine or butter
2 teaspoons finely grated orange peel
2 tablespoons orange juice

Divide asparagus spears among 6 salad plates. Stir egg yolks, yogurt and lemon juice in 1-quart saucepan briskly with wooden spoon. Add ¼ cup of the margarine. Heat over very low heat, stirring constantly, until margarine is melted. Add remaining ¼ cup margarine; continue stirring briskly until margarine is melted and sauce thickened. (Be sure margarine melts slowly; this gives eggs time to cook and thicken sauce without curdling.) Remove from heat; stir in orange peel and juice. Serve warm over asparagus spears.

Spinach-Avocado Salad

8 SERVINGS

¼ cup sesame seed
Avocado Dressing (below)
10 ounces spinach, torn into bite-size
   pieces
2 hard-cooked eggs, chopped
1 small onion, thinly sliced and
   separated into rings
½ medium avocado, cut into ½-inch
   pieces
1 hard-cooked egg, sliced

Toast sesame seed in ungreased shallow pan in 350° oven, stirring occasionally, until golden, 8 to 10 minutes. Prepare Avocado Dressing; toss with spinach, chopped eggs, onion, avocado and sesame seed. Garnish with egg slices.

AVOCADO DRESSING

½ medium avocado
2 to 3 tablespoons lemon juice
¼ cup vegetable oil
½ teaspoon salt
Dash of pepper

Mash avocado with lemon juice; stir in the remaining ingredients.

Greek Salad

8 ounces green beans
3 small zucchini, cut into ½-inch slices
1 small cauliflower, separated into
  flowerets
½ cup olive or vegetable oil
¼ cup lemon juice
1 teaspoon salt
½ teaspoon sugar
½ teaspoon dried oregano leaves
1 clove garlic, finely chopped
Lettuce leaves
1 small onion, sliced and separated into
  rings
Cherry tomatoes, cut into halves
Ripe olives

Heat 1 inch salted water (½ teaspoon salt to 1 cup water) to boiling in 3-quart saucepan. Add beans. Heat to boiling; reduce heat. Cover and simmer 5 minutes. Add zucchini and cauliflower. Heat to boiling; reduce heat. Cover and simmer just until tender, about 5 minutes; drain.

Place cooked vegetables in shallow dish. Mix oil, lemon juice, salt, sugar, oregano and garlic; pour over vegetables. Cover and refrigerate, spooning marinade over vegetables occasionally, at least 2 hours.

Just before serving, remove vegetables to lettuce-lined plates with slotted spoon; top with onion rings. Garnish with cherry tomatoes and olives. Sprinkle a few tablespoonfuls of crumbled feta cheese over each salad before serving, if desired.

Pickled Eggs on Greens

6 hard-cooked eggs, peeled
1 cup cider vinegar
1 cup beet liquid
⅓ cup granulated or packed brown
  sugar
½ teaspoon salt
1 small onion, chopped (about ¼ cup)
4 whole cloves
Shredded salad greens

Place eggs in glass bowl or jar. Mix remaining ingredients except greens; pour over eggs. Cover and refrigerate to blend flavors, at least 2 days. Cut eggs crosswise into slices; serve on greens.

Following pages: Greek Salad

Cream of Almond Soup

1 tablespoon margarine or butter
1 tablespoon all-purpose flour
½ teaspoon salt
⅛ teaspoon pepper
1 can (10¾ ounces) condensed chicken
    broth
2 cups half-and-half
⅓ cup toasted sliced almonds
½ teaspoon grated lemon peel

Heat margarine in 1½-quart saucepan over low heat until melted. Stir in flour, salt and pepper. Cook over low heat, stirring constantly, until smooth and bubbly; remove from heat. Stir in broth. Heat to boiling, stirring constantly. Boil and stir 1 minute; reduce heat. Stir in remaining ingredients; heat just until soup is hot.

Savory Consommé

2½ cups water
2 beef bouillon cubes
    or 2 teaspoons instant beef bouillon
1½ teaspoons prepared horseradish
1 teaspoon lemon juice
¼ teaspoon dried dill weed
5 thin lemon slices

Heat all ingredients except lemon slices to boiling, stirring occasionally. Garnish with lemon slices.

Cold Cucumber and Yogurt Soup

7 SERVINGS (ABOUT ½ CUP EACH)

2 medium cucumbers
1½ cups plain yogurt
½ teaspoon salt
¼ teaspoon dried mint flakes
⅛ teaspoon white pepper

Cut 7 thin slices from 1 cucumber; reserve. Cut remaining cucumber into ¾-inch chunks. Place half of the cucumber chunks and ¼ cup of the yogurt in blender container. Cover and blend on high speed until smooth. Add remaining cucumber (except reserved slices), the salt, mint and pepper. Cover and blend on low speed until smooth. Add remaining yogurt; cover and blend on low speed until smooth. Cover and refrigerate until chilled, at least 1 hour. Garnish with reserved cucumber slices and sprigs of fresh mint, if desired.

Rigatoni with Pesto Sauce

8 SERVINGS

1 package (16 ounces) rigatoni
Pesto Sauce (below)

Cook rigatoni as directed; drain. Prepare Pesto Sauce; pour over hot rigatoni. Toss until well coated. Serve with grated Parmesan cheese, if desired.

PESTO SAUCE

2 cups firmly packed fresh basil leaves
¾ cup grated Parmesan cheese
¾ cup olive oil
2 tablespoons pine nuts
4 cloves garlic

Place all ingredients in blender container. Cover and blend on medium speed, stopping blender occasionally to scrape sides, until smooth, about 3 minutes.

Note: Pesto Sauce can be kept frozen no longer than 6 months. To serve, let stand at room temperature until thawed, at least 4 hours.

Fettuccine with Four Cheeses

¼ cup margarine or butter
½ cup half-and-half
½ cup shredded Gruyère cheese
¼ cup grated Parmesan cheese
½ teaspoon salt
⅛ teaspoon freshly ground pepper
1 clove garlic, finely chopped
8 ounces uncooked fettuccine
2 tablespoons olive oil
½ cup crumbled Gorgonzola cheese
½ cup shredded mozzarella cheese
1 tablespoon snipped parsley

Heat margarine and half-and-half in 2-quart saucepan over low heat until margarine is melted. Stir in Gruyère cheese, Parmesan cheese, salt, pepper and garlic. Cook 5 minutes, stirring occasionally.

Cook fettuccine as directed on package, except add oil to boiling water; drain. Add hot fettuccine to sauce; add Gorgonzola cheese and mozzarella cheese. Toss with two forks until mixed; sprinkle with parsley.

SWEET SNACKS

Honey-Nut Bran Muffins

3 JUMBO, 5 LARGE OR 6 MEDIUM MUFFINS

$1/4$ cup natural bran
3 tablespoons boiling water
1 egg
$1/4$ cup milk
2 tablespoons vegetable oil
$2/3$ cup all-purpose flour
$1/4$ cup chopped nuts
2 tablespoons packed dark brown sugar
2 tablespoons honey
$1 1/2$ teaspoons baking powder
Dash of salt

Heat oven to 400°. Grease bottoms only of three 6-ounce custard cups, 5 large muffin cups, $3 \times 1 1/4$ inches, or 6 medium muffin cups, $2 1/2 \times 1 1/4$ inches.

Mix bran and water. Beat egg in large bowl; stir in milk and oil. Stir in bran mixture and remaining ingredients just until flour is moistened. Divide batter among cups (cups will be almost full). Place custard cups on cookie sheet. Bake until golden brown, custard cups about 25 minutes, muffin cups 20 to 25 minutes. Remove immediately from cups.

Note: After baking, seal muffins in plastic bags and freeze up to 3 months.

Oat-Peach Muffins

1 cup quick-cooking oats
1 cup buttermilk
¼ cup vegetable oil
2 tablespoons light molasses
1 teaspoon vanilla
1 egg
1¼ cups all-purpose flour
¾ cup ¼-inch pieces fresh peaches*
¾ cup coarsely chopped walnuts
¼ cup packed brown sugar
1½ teaspoons ground cinnamon
1 teaspoon baking soda
1 teaspoon baking powder
½ teaspoon salt

Heat oven to 400°. Grease bottoms only of six 6-ounce custard cups, 10 large muffin cups, 3 × 1¼ inches, or 12 medium muffin cups, 2½ × 1¼ inches.

Mix oats and buttermilk in large bowl; beat in oil, molasses, vanilla and egg with fork. Stir in remaining ingredients just until flour is moistened. Divide batter among cups (cups will be full). Place custard cups on cookie sheet. Bake until wooden pick inserted in center comes out clean, custard cups 20 to 25 minutes, muffin cups 15 to 20 minutes. Remove immediately from cups.

*Canned peaches, well drained, or frozen peaches, thawed and well drained, can be used.

OAT-DATE MUFFINS: Substitute chopped dates for the peaches.

OAT-RAISIN MUFFINS: Substitute raisins for the peaches.

Banana Bread

1 cup sugar
1/3 cup margarine or butter, softened
2 eggs
1 1/2 cups mashed ripe bananas (3 to 4
  medium)
1/3 cup water
1 2/3 cups all-purpose flour
1 teaspoon baking soda
1/2 teaspoon salt
1/4 teaspoon baking powder
1/2 cup chopped nuts

Heat oven to 350°. Grease bottom only of loaf pan, 8 1/2 × 4 1/2 × 2 1/2 or 9 × 5 × 3 inches. Mix sugar and margarine in 2 1/2-quart bowl. Stir in eggs until blended. Add bananas and water; beat 30 seconds. Stir in remaining ingredients except nuts until just moistened; stir in nuts. Pour into pan. Bake until wooden pick inserted in center comes out clean, 8-inch loaf 1 1/4 hours, 9-inch loaf 55 to 60 minutes; cool 5 minutes. Loosen sides of loaf from pan; remove from pan. Cool completely before slicing.

NOTE: Wrap and refrigerate no longer than 1 week.

Apple-Raisin Bread

3 cups chopped unpared apples
3 cups all-purpose flour
2 1/2 cups sugar
1 1/4 cups vegetable oil
4 eggs, beaten
1 tablespoon plus 1 teaspoon vanilla
2 teaspoons ground cinnamon
1 1/2 teaspoons salt
1 1/2 teaspoons baking soda
1 teaspoon ground cloves
1/2 teaspoon baking powder
2/3 cup raisins
1/2 cup chopped nuts

Heat oven to 325°. Generously grease bottoms only of 2 loaf pans, 9 × 5 × 3 inches. Beat all ingredients on low speed, scraping bowl constantly, 1 minute. Beat on medium speed 1 minute. Pour into pans. Bake until wooden pick inserted in center comes out clean, about 1 hour. Cool 10 minutes; remove from pans. Cool completely before slicing. Store in refrigerator.

ZUCCHINI BREAD: Substitute 4 cups coarsely shredded zucchini for the apples. Omit raisins and increase nuts to 1 cup.

Scones

1/3 cup margarine or butter
1 3/4 cups all-purpose flour
3 tablespoons sugar
2 1/2 teaspoons baking powder
1/2 teaspoon salt
1 egg, beaten
1/2 cup currants or raisins
4 to 6 tablespoons half-and-half
1 egg, beaten

Heat oven to 400°. Cut margarine into flour, sugar, baking powder and salt with pastry blender until mixture resembles fine crumbs. Stir in 1 egg, the currants and just enough half-and-half so dough leaves side of bowl.

Turn dough onto lightly floured surface. Knead lightly 10 times. Roll or pat 1/2 inch thick. Cut with floured 2-inch round cutter, or cut into diamond shapes with sharp knife. Place on ungreased cookie sheet; brush dough with 1 egg. Bake until golden brown, 10 to 12 minutes. Remove immediately from cookie sheet; cool. Split scones. Serve with strawberry preserves, if desired.

Chutney Quick Bread

2 1/2 cups all-purpose flour
1/2 cup granulated sugar
1/2 cup packed brown sugar
1 1/4 cups milk
3 tablespoons vegetable oil
1 tablespoon grated orange peel
3 1/2 teaspoons baking powder
1 teaspoon salt
1 egg
1 cup chopped nuts
3/4 cup mild chutney
Spreads (page 93)

Heat oven to 350°. Grease a loaf pan, 9 × 5 × 3 inches. Mix flour, sugars, milk, oil, orange peel, baking powder, salt and egg in large bowl. Beat on low speed, scraping bowl constantly, until moistened. Beat on medium speed 30 seconds, scraping bowl occasionally. Stir in nuts and chutney. Pour into pan. Bake until wooden pick inserted in center comes out clean, 60 to 65 minutes. Cool slightly; remove from pan. Cool completely on wire rack. Serve with one of the spreads.

LEMON–CREAM CHEESE SPREAD

1 CUP

*1 package (8 ounces) cream cheese,
  softened*
1 tablespoon powdered sugar
1 teaspoon grated lemon peel
1 tablespoon lemon juice

Beat all ingredients on medium speed until
fluffy.

WHIPPED HONEY–ORANGE BUTTER

1 CUP

1 cup margarine or butter, softened
2 tablespoons honey
2 teaspoons grated orange peel

Beat all ingredients on medium speed until
fluffy.

CURRIED SPREAD

1 CUP

*1 package (8 ounces) cream cheese,
  softened*
2 teaspoons sugar
2 teaspoons curry powder
Dash of salt

Beat all ingredients until smooth.

FRUITED CREAM CHEESE SPREAD

1 ¼ CUPS

*1 package (8 ounces) cream cheese,
  softened*
*¼ cup peach or apricot preserves or
  orange marmalade*

Beat cream cheese and preserves or marmalade
on medium speed until fluffy.

*Following pages: Chutney Quick Bread with Fruited Cream Cheese
Spread and Lemon–Cream Cheese Spread*

RED SPOON TIPS

Serving Appetizers

Many appetizers, small by nature, are destined to be attractive. With just a little attention and loving care, any hors d'oeuvre can be a real knockout.

Here are some Red Spoon Tips to make your appetizers look like blue-ribbon winners:

- Emphasize the beauty of assembled hors d'oeuvres by neatly arranging them on plain white china plates (unless the food is white) or polished silver or lacquered trays. Space the food generously. Party Sandwiches, Mexican Deviled Eggs and Crab Roll-ups with Avocado Dip, for example, show to great advantage on these surfaces.
- Bravura appetizers such as Brie in Crust benefit from similar simple treatment. Serve them where they can be admired and guests can easily help themselves.
- What to do with appetizers like dips? If they are colorful, serve in a plain bowl. Some appetizers are utterly delicious, but dull to look at, so serve them in brilliantly colored glazed ceramics, bright majolica or some of the ornately patterned, inexpensive Oriental export china.

- The origin of some foods can suggest serving ideas. Guacamole, Salsa Roja and Salsa Verde are naturals for Southwestern-style pottery. Then, toss tortilla chips in a basket or wooden bowl lined with a bright cloth or bandanna and bring on the guests.

Decorating Hints

Garnishes have a life beyond parsley. Fresh herbs look sensational, especially when they garnish foods they flavor. For a rustic look, bundle them into a little spray or nosegay; for a more elegant look, scatter or tuck the leaves and blossoms around the food. (See page 6 in the Introduction for additional garnishing ideas.)

Don't be shy about using canapé or small cookie cutters. Thinly sliced breads and cucumber slices make exceptional bases for creamy fillings when cut into diminutive hearts, diamonds or flowers.

Chives are ideal for tying around cooked shrimp and Crab Roll-ups, snipping and showering over pale spreads and crisscrossing on open-face sandwiches.

Decorate tidbits topped by a creamy spread with any of the following: tiny sliced cornichons (pickles), edible flower petals, chopped pistachio nuts, several alfalfa sprouts, slivers of red or yellow bell peppers, paper-thin rings of jalapeño peppers, pine nuts toasted or raw, or dots of bright jam or chutney—your imagination is the limit. These little touches are just as nice for dressing up vegetables as they are for topping crackers. Stuffed endive leaves, rounds of radish, cucumber or summer squash slices spread with dip all shine with that extra accent, as small as it seems.

A pastry bag can be one of your best friends in the kitchen. With just three tips and ten minutes of practice, you can create charming appetizers. Piping decorations works best with a medium-firm mixture of uniform texture. A cream cheese mixture studded with chopped bits would not pipe as successfully as one with a flavoring beaten smoothly in. Mock Pâté de Foie Gras, any of the cream cheeses for the Party Sandwiches, Lemon–Cream Cheese Spread, Curry Spread and Fruited Cream Cheese Spread would work well. Pipe savory mixtures onto fruits and vegetables, cold cuts and crackers and sweet ones onto split scones and neat quick-bread squares.

Cheese mixtures are difficult to pipe straight from the refrigerator—too firm—and should be allowed to warm slightly. Too warm, however, and they don't hold their shape nicely and look greasy. Fill the pastry bag one-third to halfway full and twist the open end of the bag closed. Exert even pressure on the mixture in the bag with one hand, directing the tip with the other hand.

If the mixture gets too soft while you are working, set the pastry bag in the refrigerator for a few minutes until the mixture is of the proper consistency again.

Entertaining

It is usually a good idea to list items needed for a party and plan the time necessary to assemble them. Make a grocery list and a separate list of such things as napkins (plan on two or three times as many napkins as guests), wooden picks, candles, ashtrays, bamboo skewers, plastic glasses and the like. Nonperishable items may be purchased far in advance.

Three days before the party: Follow up on any truant R.S.V.P.s. Finalize the party menu and budget. Check that any equipment needed is at hand. For the bar, this may include corkscrew, can/bottle opener, ice bucket, ice tongs, citrus zester, small sharp knife, small cutting board, jigger, stirrers and small dishes to hold garnishes.

One day before the party: Purchase dry goods. Prepare any foods that can be made ahead of time. Imagine what food will be served in which dishes, and lay out the food arrangement in your mind (or on paper, if it helps to keep you organized). Borrow serving dishes, if you discover you are short. Confirm any arrangements made with the florist. And if there is any housecleaning to be done, this is the time to do it.

The day of the party: Purchase fresh produce and other perishable goods. Make ice cubes if arrangements haven't been made for ice delivery (if they have, confirm delivery). Prepare the remaining foods. Jot down a timetable of the foods to be cooked or warmed. Arrange the food, lighting and decorations—and then enjoy yourself.

Party Emergencies

As host or hostess, it is not always easy to keep a level head. Here are some solutions to typical party emergencies:

A mountain of ice has been delivered, but the ice bucket holds just two pounds. Solution: If the ice is still in the delivery bags stash it in the bathtub. Refill the ice bucket as needed. Bonus: Tuck bottles of mixers, beer and white wine securely among the bags of ice to chill, freeing refrigerator space.

One batch of appetizers is left to burn in the oven, another is spilled onto the floor, and hungry guests have eaten everything set out for them. Solution: From a well-stocked pantry shelf, pull down cans of nuts or popping corn and refer to some of these Red Spoon recipes:

Parmesan-glazed Walnuts, Ginger Almonds, Oriental-style Nuts or Parmesan-Curry Popcorn. Empty a jar of good-quality olives into a pretty dish and set it out; no one will know you didn't have time to marinate them.

In the course of the evening, a guest becomes inebriated. Solution: Ask a good friend to help you by seeing the guest safely home. Alternatively, tuck the guest into a taxi cab. If the guest is inclined to refuse assistance, be very firm.

Refrigerator space runs out just when the salmon mousse needs to be chilled. Solution: A neighbor might be able to lend you some room in her refrigerator. If that isn't possible, take anything that isn't perishable out of the refrigerator and set it aside temporarily.

A quarrel develops between two guests. Solution: It is the responsibility of the host or hostess to ensure harmony. Try to interrupt the dispute gracefully, without drawing attention to it, and steer one of the angry guests off to join another conversation on the other side of the room.

Party Menus

COCKTAILS AT 8:
A WINTER MENU   SERVES 8

- Mini Oriental Rolls
- Ginger Almonds
- Brie in Crust
- Curried Shrimp with Flatbread
- Parmesan Fans

COCKTAILS AT 8:
A SUMMER MENU   SERVES 8

- Ginger Dip with Apples and Pears
- Cucumber-Shrimp Party Sandwiches (2 per guest)
- Chive and Feta Cheese Triangles
- Jícama Appetizer
- Parmesan-glazed Walnuts

OPEN HOUSE APPETIZER
BUFFET   SERVES 25

- Cheese Board: Montrachet, an American blue-veined cheese, L'Explorateur and Cheddar—served with a variety of sliced breads
- Marinated Mushrooms
- Ginger Shrimp
- Spinach Dip with endive, cucumber and radish dippers
- Cajun Crabmeat Mold with rye crackers
- Italian Sausage Terrine with assorted crackers
- Onion-Cheese Puffs
- Parmesan-Curry Popcorn

RAINY DAY FOOTBALL:
A TV PARTY   SERVES 8

- Cereal Corn Snack
- Chili Quiche Appetizers
- Deviled Ham and Mushroom Spread with pumpernickel bread
- Kielbasa in Fondue
- Selection of crudités

CASUAL GET-TOGETHER   SERVES 10

- Eggplant Dip with carrot and zucchini stick dippers
- Salmon Mousse with toasted, sliced baguettes
- Cheese and Apple Toasts
- Garlic Olives

TAILGATE PICNIC   SERVES 4

- Chutney Spread with assorted crackers
- Mock Pâté de Foie Gras with sliced baguettes
- Chinese-style Barbecued Ribs
- Dilled Vegetables
- Banana Bread

Beverages for Parties

Planning drinks for a dinner party differs from planning cocktails for a cocktail party. At the dinner table, guests drink what is placed before them. At a cocktail party, they select (or even prepare for themselves) what they would like to drink. It is nice to offer a selection, yet choosing what to offer can be confusing. What host wants to be left at the end of a party with bottles of aperitifs or liquors that no one was tempted to open?

For a 1½- to 2-hour party for 12 guests, use the list below as a guide. Of course your guests won't drink every drop—and they're not meant to—but the quantities should provide enough of those drinks people favor most often.

2 bottles dry white wine
2 bottles red wine
1 fifth dry sherry
1 small bottle dry vermouth
1 quart vodka
1 quart Scotch, bourbon or rye whisky
1 fifth gin
1 fifth light or golden rum
2 quarts mineral water
2 quarts tonic water
1 quart ginger ale
1 quart cola
2 quarts club soda
10 to 15 pounds ice

To serve 25, double the quantities of white wine, red wine, vodka and the mixers.

Set out a fifth of vermouth and a quart each of gin and rum. Select two additional bottles of whisky. Buy twenty-five to thirty pounds of ice.

If a guest has a special fondness for Campari, Dubonnet, fruit juices or the like, it would be thoughtful to provide some. Certainly if the party is casual, or takes place in sultry weather, cold beer would be refreshing. For a late morning or early afternoon party, stock some tomato juice for Bloody Marys, along with red pepper sauce, prepared horseradish and freshly ground pepper. Don't forget to put out little dishes of lemons and limes cut into wedges and cocktail olives or onions (or both). And for guests who enjoy a bracing cup of coffee, brew a fresh pot and keep it where they can serve themselves.

Nothing is easier on the host than serving punch. It is simply a matter of mixing the chilled ingredients. Punch cups hold approximately 4 ounces, and guests will probably have 3 servings in the course of a 1½- to 2-hour party; thus, figure about 12 ounces per guest.

Champagne punches are gala, but bear in mind that an expensive champagne or sparkling wine is not at its best in a punch. Pour champagne and carbonated mixers into the punch bowl slowly, letting the liquid run down the side of the bowl rather than splashing into the center; that way, much of the effervescence is preserved. Add carbonated beverages just before serving, so they don't lose their "fizz." Punch is a fine old European institution, and there are literally hundreds of delicious recipes. Don't forget to taste your punch, though, and adjust it to taste.

Keep punch cold by adding ice as it melts during the party. An ice ring will melt more slowly than ice cubes. To make an ice ring, fill a ring mold with water and freeze it. Dip the mold into hot water to release the ice. If you want, you can decorate your ice ring. Just pour an inch or two of water into the mold and freeze. Arrange citrus slices, cranberries, small strawberries, raspberries, mint leaves or green grapes on the frozen ring and fill with water and then freeze.

Finally, a trick to keep mixed drinks cold without diluting them too much: Make "ice cubes" using tonic water, ginger ale or cola, and use them in place of plain tap water ice cubes.

About Cheese

A selection of cheeses is an easy and handsome addition to any hors d'oeuvres. Remember, however, that people will nibble on cheese as long as it lasts. So, if you are serving dinner and want your guests to still have an appetite when they sit down for the meal, plan on an ounce or two of cheese per person.

Serve cheese with thinly sliced breads and crackers. In the bread category, you might try pumpernickel, Swedish limpa rye or Italian or French baguettes. As for crackers, you can buy an assortment especially made for serving with cheese and vary the offering even more with Scandinavian flatbreads, rice crackers and whole-grain biscuits. It is nice to serve an assortment of crudités (raw vegetables, washed, trimmed and cut into bite-size pieces if necessary), as well.

A good rule of thumb for putting together a cheese board is to assemble three or four different kinds of cheese: mild, sharp, soft and blue-veined, for example. A simple selection might begin with Gruyère, Cheddar, Saint-André and Gorgonzola.

CHEESE	COUNTRY OF ORIGIN	DESCRIPTION	USE
SOFT			
Bel Paese	Italy	mild, sweet, creamy	snack, dessert, cooking
Brie	France	mild to pungent	snack, dessert
Camembert	France	mild to pungent	snack, dessert
Montrachet	France	mild	salads, cooking, snack
Triple Crèmes: Brillat-Savarin L'Explorateur Saint-André	France	mild, creamy	snack, dessert
SEMISOFT			
Feta	Greece	sharp, salty, crumbly	salads, cooking
Mozzarella	Italy	mild	snack, cooking
Muenster	Germany	mild to sharp	snack, dessert
Port du Salut	France	mild to robust	snack, dessert
FIRM			
Cheddar	England	mild to very sharp	snack, dessert, cooking
Cheshire	England	crumbly, ripe	snack, cooking
Edam and Gouda	Holland	mild, nutty	snack, dessert, cooking
Fontina	Italy	mellow, nutty	snack, dessert, cooking
Gjetost	Norway	sweet, caramel	snack, dessert, cooking
Gruyère	Switzerland	nutty, mild to sharp	snack, dessert, cooking
Monterey Jack	U.S.A.	mild	snack, cooking
Provolone	Italy	mild to sharp, smoky	snack, cooking
Swiss (Emmanthaler)	Switzerland	mild, nutty	snack, dessert, cooking
HARD			
Kashkaval	Yugoslavia	salty	snack, dessert
Parmesan	Italy	sharp, piquant	snack, cooking
Romano	Italy	sharp, piquant	cooking
BLUE-VEINED			
Bleu	Denmark	tangy, sharp, firm	snack, dessert, salads
Gorgonzola	Italy	piquant, creamy	snack, dessert, salads
Roquefort	France	sharp, piquant, semisoft	snack, dessert, salads
Stilton	England	mild, piquant, semisoft	snack, dessert

First Courses

Serving a first course doesn't have to mean a great deal of extra effort. In fact, a first course can be as simple as a glass of chilled fruit juice. What a first course does, though, is add a festive note, making the most of those special occasions we are reluctant to see come to an end. It makes for a heartier meal, too.

When setting the table for a meal that includes a first course, consider what you are serving and the silverware it calls for. Parmesan Oysters, for example, call for a special seafood fork or other small fork. That fork would lie to the left of the other fork(s) at the place setting. If serving Cream of Almond Soup, add a soup spoon to the place setting to the right of the teaspoon. If a fresh Greek Salad opens the meal, place a salad fork to the left of the dinner fork.

First courses have a reputation for formality. It may come as a surprise that not all first courses must be enjoyed in the dining room. There's no reason that juice or soup can't be sipped outdoors on the lawn, if the weather is balmy, or at a cheery fireside before the main course is served at the table. And, of course, many of the "finger food" appetizers in this book do double duty as first courses, too. Consider some of the following choices:

- Ginger Shrimp (page 46): 7 or 8 shrimp make an ample serving
- Shrimp Toast (page 47): serve 3 or 4 toasts
- Escabeche (page 51): $1/3$ to $1/2$ cup is sufficient
- Dilled Vegetables (page 60): serve about $1/2$ cup
- Mini Oriental Rolls (page 71): serve 2 rolls

Snacks, American-style

We Americans like our snacks good and *crunchy*, whether they are savory or sweet. And because we can't seem to get enough of them, here are four additional super-crunchy snacks to enjoy by the handful. They make great take-along treats, too!

Golden Peanut Snack

ABOUT 6 CUPS

5 cups honey graham cereal
1 cup salted peanuts
¼ cup creamy peanut butter
2 tablespoons margarine or butter
1 teaspoon ground cinnamon
1 cup raisins

Heat oven to 350°. Mix cereal and peanuts in large bowl. Heat peanut butter, margarine and cinnamon in 1-quart saucepan over low heat, stirring until blended. Pour over cereal and peanuts, stirring until coated. Spread in ungreased rectangular baking pan, 13 × 9 × 2 inches. Bake, stirring occasionally, 15 minutes. Stir in raisins; spread on waxed paper. Let stand at least 2 hours.

Sweet and Crunchy Cereal Snack

ABOUT 8 CUPS

4 cups crispy corn puff cereal
1 cup Spanish peanuts
1 cup raisins
1 cup dried banana chips
3 tablespoons margarine or butter
3 tablespoons honey
¾ teaspoon ground cinnamon
½ teaspoon salt
1 cup flaked coconut

Heat oven to 325°. Mix cereal, peanuts, raisins and banana chips in ungreased jelly roll pan, 15½ × 10½ × 1 inch. Heat margarine and honey in 1-quart saucepan over low heat until margarine is melted. Stir in cinnamon and salt; pour over cereal mixture, tossing until evenly coated. Bake 15 minutes, stirring once. Stir in coconut. Let stand 5 minutes; loosen from pan. Sprinkle with additional salt, if desired.

Nutty O's

1/2 cup packed brown sugar
1/2 cup dark corn syrup
1/4 cup margarine or butter
1/2 teaspoon salt
6 cups toasted oat cereal
1 cup pecan halves, walnut halves or
    peanuts
1/2 cup slivered almonds

Heat oven to 325°. Grease jelly roll pan, 15 1/2 × 10 1/2 × 1 inch. Heat brown sugar, corn syrup, margarine and salt in 3-quart saucepan over medium heat, stirring constantly, until sugar is dissolved, about 5 minutes; remove from heat. Stir in cereal and nuts until well coated. Spread mixture in pan. Bake 15 minutes. Cool 10 minutes; loosen mixture with metal spatula. Let stand until firm, about 1 hour. Store in covered container.

Oven Caramel Corn

3 quarts (12 cups) popped corn
1 cup packed brown sugar
1/2 cup margarine or butter
1/4 cup light corn syrup
1/2 teaspoon salt
1/2 teaspoon baking soda

Heat oven to 200°. Divide popped corn between 2 ungreased rectangular baking pans, 13 × 9 × 2 inches. Heat sugar, margarine, corn syrup and salt, stirring occasionally, until bubbly around edges. Continue cooking over medium heat 5 minutes.

Remove from heat; stir in baking soda until foamy. Pour on popped corn, stirring until corn is well coated. Bake 1 hour, stirring every 15 minutes.

Pantry List

With a good selection of groceries from the following list on hand, delicious appetizers, snacks and first courses are ready for the fixing. In addition to such pantry staples as salt, whole peppercorns for grinding fresh pepper, vegetable oil, olive oil, vinegar, cornstarch, baking powder and baking soda, keep some fresh produce in stock, such as onions, heads of garlic, lemons and limes. Then choose from the following:

HERBS AND SPICES

- Garlic powder
- Garlic salt
- Dried basil
- Dried thyme leaves
- Dried dill weed
- Dry mustard
- Dried tarragon leaves
- Dried oregano leaves
- Ground ginger
- Ground cinnamon
- Ground allspice
- Ground nutmeg
- Ground cloves
- Red pepper flakes
- Chili powder
- Onion powder
- Curry powder
- Five-spice powder

CONDIMENTS AND SAUCES

- Worcestershire sauce
- Mayonnaise
- Prepared horseradish
- Chutney
- Red pepper sauce
- Soy sauce
- Prepared mustard
- Chili sauce

DAIRY GOODS

- Cream cheese
- Dairy sour cream
- Cottage cheese
- Plain yogurt
- Cheddar cheese

PANTRY SHELF

- Crackers (keep an assortment on hand)
- Nuts: walnut halves, peanuts (Spanish, salted), sliced almonds, whole almonds, dry-roasted mixed nuts
- Ripe olives
- Green olives
- Deviled ham (canned)
- Crabmeat (canned)
- Small shrimp (canned)
- Salmon (canned)
- Popcorn
- Variety baking mix
- Raisins or currants
- Honey
- Water chestnuts (canned)

Kitchen Equipment

If you have a good selection of tools from the lists below, you will find it easy to turn out appetizers, snacks and first courses like a professional. Sometimes one piece of equipment can do the work of another; a fine mesh sieve can serve in place of a sifter, and food processor shredding and grating attachments can do the work of a grater.

BASIC EQUIPMENT

- Assorted canapé cutters or small cookie cutters
- Blender
- Baking sheets (shiny, aluminum variety)
- Colander
- Cooling racks
- Crocks or ramekins
- Fine mesh sieve
- Grater
- Kitchen knives (sharp)
- Loaf pan (9 × 5 × 3 or 8½ × 4½ × 2½ inches)

- Measuring cups (both liquid measuring cups and graduated measuring cups)
- Measuring spoons
- Melon ball cutter
- Mold, metal or ceramic (4-cup)
- Muffin tins (cups 3 × 1¼ or 2½ × 1½ inches)
- Pans: square (9 × 9 × 2 inches), rectangular (13 × 9 × 2 inches) and jelly roll pan (15½ × 10½ × 1 inch)
- Pepper mill
- Pie plates (8 × 1¼ and 9 × 1¼ inches)
- Rolling pin
- Rubber spatula
- Sifter
- Vegetable peeler
- Wooden spoons

OPTIONAL EQUIPMENT

- Custard cups
- Electric mixer
- Food processor
- Pastry bag with assorted tips
- 12-inch pizza pan

INDEX

Credits

V.P., Associate Publisher: Anne M. Zeman
Project Editor: Rebecca W. Atwater
Creative Director: J.C. Suarès
Photographer: Anthony Johnson
Designer: Patricia Fabricant
Production Editor: Kimberly Ebert

WORTH
20 COUPON POINTS

For Betty Crocker Catalog, send 50¢ (no stamps) with your name and address to: General Mills, Box 59078, Minneapolis, MN 55459. Redeemable with cash by U.S. purchaser of product before April, 1999. Void where prohibited, taxed or regulated.

S

BETTY CROCKER COUPON